Henri Didon, Raphaël Ledos de Beaufort

The Germans

Henri Didon, Raphaël Ledos de Beaufort

The Germans

ISBN/EAN: 9783742894731

Hergestellt in Europa, USA, Kanada, Australien, Japan

Cover: Foto ©ninafisch / pixelio.de

Manufactured and distributed by brebook publishing software (www.brebook.com)

Henri Didon, Raphaël Ledos de Beaufort

The Germans

BY THE

REV. FATHER DIDON

OF THE ORDER OF PREACHING FRIARS

TRANSLATED INTO ENGLISH

BY

RAPHAËL LEDOS DE BEAUFORT, LL.B.

WILLIAM BLACKWOOD AND SONS
EDINBURGH AND LONDON
MDCCCLXXXIV

APPROBATION OF THE ORDER.

By the command of the Very Rev. Father Faucillon, Provincial Director of the Preaching Friars of the province of France, we have examined the work of the Rev. Father Didon, entitled 'The Germans.'

We consider it worthy of publication.

Fr. PAUL MONJARDET,
Preacher-General.

Fr. CESLAS BAYONNE,
Bachelor of Divinity.

PARIS, *December* 1882.

Imprimatur—

Fr. THOMAS FAUCILLON,
Provincial Director.

PREFACE.

As the result of personal observation, this work, notwithstanding unavoidable shortcomings, may afford some interest to the reader.

That which I have seen, I describe faithfully; that which I have felt, I frankly express. Neither in her press, the organ of public opinion, nor still less in her foreign policy, does Germany conceal her implacable hostility to France. I, nevertheless, wish to speak of her without disparagement, as I endeavour to judge my own country without flattery, and without self-deception.

Passionately loving France, I wish to serve her dispassionately.

I know her worth, and am heartily ambitious of her glory and her primacy. The misfortunes

of my country, her disasters, her faults even,
have not caused me to doubt of her.   My
patriotism has preserved my faith in her providential mission ; and the unparalleled convulsions of the century through which she has
just passed have not destroyed one atom of my
hope in her future.

December 1883.

TRANSLATOR'S PREFACE.

In the present strained relations existing between Great Britain and Germany, a careful
and impartial study of the manifold causes
which brought to life and developed the out-
burst of national activity that resulted in the
unity of Germany and the creation of the
mighty Empire which has so suddenly risen in
Central Europe, and so powerfully disturbed
the European equilibrium, may not be devoid
of interest for the British public. This is why
I now take the liberty of bringing before them
the translation of a work which, on the Continent, is causing quite a sensation. Though
a Frenchman, Father Didon's judgment and
power of observation have not been prejudiced
by his patriotism, an error so common nowa-

days; and though relating to an enemy, his observations are throughout just, devoid of chauvinism (that great plague of international relations, too often, alas! mistaken for patriotism), and not likely to give umbrage to any impartial judge.

As regards the translation itself, I have endeavoured, to the best of my ability, to convey in their entirety the observations and the criticisms of the author, my aim being to secure a faithful rendering of the author's work, as far as lay in my power as a foreigner ; and though the literary merits of my translation may be few, I sincerely trust the public will grant me their indulgence, which I humbly request.

I think it but just to mention, that in my undertaking I have been greatly assisted by my friend Mr P. Varnals.

RAPHAËL LEDOS DE BEAUFORT.

LONDON, *October* 1884.

CONTENTS.

V.

VI.

VII.

VIII.

IX.

XVIII.

XIX.

XX.

XXI.

XXII.

APPENDICES.

THE GERMANS.

I.

DEPARTURE FOR GERMANY—MODERN CRITICISM—MATRICULATION
  IN BERLIN UNIVERSITY—PATRIOTIC DUTY OF PUBLISHING
  THESE OBSERVATIONS.

In 1881, living in absolute seclusion, I applied myself during many a long day to the study of the origin of Christianity. He who to-day attempts such a study, is, at the same time, carried away into modern criticism as into the midst of the stormy ocean. Everything leads him thither—the laws of historical science, the study of tradition, the control of original documents.

Nowhere during the last century has modern criticism, in its bearings upon Christianity, been more patiently and more obstinately cultivated (though perhaps not so clearly and successfully as elsewhere)

A

than in the universities of Germany. This fact led
me to direct my attention towards a foreign land—
a country *anti-French*.

I unhesitatingly repressed my patriotic prejudices,
and started with the resolution of sitting with German students at the feet of their professors, at
Leipzig, Göttingen, and Berlin.

German universities are truly hospitable : they
are thrown wide open to all who wish to learn,
without distinction of age, language, creed, or nationality. They are, however, closed against all
anonymous, idle amateurs. No woman crosses the
threshold.

This is what I found at Berlin, and this is what
every stranger finds who demands inscription on the
registers of *Alma Mater*.

I wrote an application to the academic Senate,
supported by a simple passport. A few days afterwards, the secretary of the university sent me a
reply. It was favourable, as it always is, unless the
Prussian police, mistrustful and often meddlesome,
suspect the applicant of being a conspirator or
Nihilist. I was summoned for a certain day, at a
certain hour, to the large hall of the university
Senate. Punctual to the day and hour, I found
myself, with my curiosity rather excited, in the
midst of more than forty students, awaiting, like

myself, their matriculation. Most of them were
Germans, several Italians and Roumanians, a few
Russians, I alone a Frenchman. We took our
places, without distinction, on chairs ranged in order
in front of a long green table, where were seated
the rector and the university judge, assisted by two
secretaries. Upon his name being called, the candidate rises, approaches the rector, announces his
Christian name and surname, mentions his nationality,
and indicates the special faculty to which he wishes
to belong. All this is entered in the chief university register. It is also recorded on a sheet of
paper, signed by the rector. This sheet is handed
to the candidate as evidence of his affiliation.[1]
When all had been interrogated and thus enrolled,
under a matriculation number, in the great army of
students, the rector quitted the green table, and
advancing towards us said :—

"Gentlemen, henceforward you will be students
of this university. Promise to honour it, as also to
honour yourselves by your conduct and application.
Swear to be faithful to its laws."

Each of us in turn then approached the rector,
and respectfully touched his right hand as a token
of fidelity. Such, in its simplicity, in its ancient
nobility, is the rite of matriculation. That touch

[1] See Appendix A.

of the hand has an air truly chivalrous: the most insignificant things become majestic when consecrated by conscience and honour.

I also in turn had to press this strange hand, for I felt that, above frontiers and nationalities, men may, without forgetting their country, meet together in peace in the worship of truth. Science is unique; like God she is universal; she knows neither the Alps, nor the Pyrenees, nor the Rhine. Whosoever serves her, works with the same heart and with the same arm for the grandeur of his country and the evolution of the human race.

A triumph, though glorious as the sun of Austerlitz, may have a sinister morrow; but a step towards truth is a good deed for ever. I am opposed to short-sighted patriotism, moulded by egotism, rancour, and hate. I desire only a patriotism restrained by justice, stimulated only by the ambitions which justice approves, and devoting itself, not to hatred of its adversaries, but to the defence and glory of its country. The one is a vice and a plague, the other a virtue. Though in the *animal kingdom*, in the hour of struggle for existence, victory is to force, in the kingdom of humanity, intelligence and conscience alone, sooner or later, ensure empire to nations.

One day I had the curiosity to open the official directory of the Berlin University, in order to see the names of the students. I there saw, to my regret, but four French names.

Always attached to home, it is only with reluctance that we go abroad.

The foreigner—English, Russian, Italian, American, German—travels the world over, and seeks a knowledge of other nations. The Frenchman, seeing no one else, will end by not even knowing himself. But I have not the heart to press this reproach; I have too strongly felt how painful it is, even for love of the truth, to pass certain frontiers, to hear the heavy step of soldiers who have vanquished us, to pass at the foot of monuments of their victories, and to mourn for one's country amongst those who have mutilated it.

In reviewing the observations made during my stay in the various States of the Empire, and, above all, in the principal universities, it seemed to me that it would not be unserviceable to communicate something of them to my fellow-citizens. Obliged to acknowledge and to point out the merit of certain of the institutions of Germany, I have not forgotten the duties of patriotism. Like every passion, it has its exigencies, and I have treated it with respect even in its umbrageous susceptibilities.

I do not say, Let us act like the Germans; I say, Let us do better. I will not say, Let us copy their universities, their schools, their army, their national spirit ; I say, Let us surpass them. We need imitate none. It is sufficient that we be faithful to our national genius ! Let us be ourselves !

But in nations, as in every individual, there is a grand and a petty side. France will only be herself when she knows how to mistrust sectarian passions, and to obey the generous aspirations which always move her, and which remain the honour of her ardent nature.

What good is there in exciting one's self against the ruins of the old world ? They are of themselves falling to pieces. Is it not more practical and grander to realise our chivalrous ideal of social justice, of wise liberty, and our ambitions of truly encyclopedic science ? From this point of view, the foreigner—particularly if he be an enemy—can sometimes give us lessons the more useful because they the better arouse our emulation, by stinging our national vanity to the quick.

Thus both patriotic interest and duty demand that we should carefully observe German life.

II.

BETWEEN France and Germany there exists a profound antagonism. A careful observer will always detect it in the reserved politeness that stamps the relations existing between Frenchmen and Germans, even in business pursuits, or on the still more peaceable ground of scientific investigation.

Thirteen years of peace have not abated it. The Rhine that flows between the two nations has become a stream of blood; and will recover its limpidity only on the day when the dreadful wound of Alsace and Lorraine shall have ceased to bleed. He, however, would be vastly mistaken who should see in such antagonism solely a question of revenge, or the opposition of races, deeply antipathetic.

Struggle for pre-eminence is the true name of the latent war which exists between Germany and France.

It involves the displacing of the centre of the

forces which direct the world, to shift it eastward; to
Berlin, to Prussia, to Germany, in the midst of the
races of the north.   That their country should take
the lead of mankind is the dream of all great patriots.

Such is the dream of Germany.

She has the ambition or the pretension of being,
in a military, political, scientific, moral, religious, and
intellectual (*cérébralement*) sense, the leading nation of
the world.   Chauvinism in Germany is more than
a sentiment—it is a theory, a scientific dogma.
There, but two races are recognised—the German
and the Latin.   As a matter of course, the German
is placed first, although the later arrival on the
scene where the leading parts are played.   With
much abstraction, philosophers formulate the system [1]
at the expense of history, the erudite attempt to
justify it, poets laud it, and the soul of the people
vibrates with the lyric accents of a Schiller.

It does not become Frenchmen to decry any national ambition.   Let them rather enlarge the circle
of their own, for there is not in history any mention
of a people whose renown was not due to the grandeur of an ideal, long cherished and ardently pursued.
Such ideal is the soul of a country.   When it leaves
them, nations die.   But whenever they are startled
by some grand idea, they commence a new evolution.

---

[1] Fichte, 'Reden an die Deutsche Nation.'

At first only caught sight of by a few eminent and far-reaching minds, the national idea inspires poets, who translate it into vibrating verse for the people ; it is hatched slowly in the brain of men of action, but when ripe, it directs events themselves, gains victories, and becomes a considerable deed in the life of mankind. The *idea* creates the *fact;* the *ideal* rules the *real.* The dream of a superior aim to be attained sets to work all men of thought and action.

How is it that German nationality, so obscure in the eighteenth century, has suddenly awaked again to consciousness? Why, so long parcelled out into small confederate states, does Germany all at once burn with the desire of overruling by her arms and by her politics, even by intellectual culture and genius, the progress of modern civilisation? It is not easy to reply. All origins are wrapped up in mystery! By the cradle of all that breathe, nations and individuals, a sphinx is seated, mute and impenetrable.

Never before were national ambitions more unduly excited. What a powerful drama in the competition and the latent or open struggle of those two modern nations! They appear like birds of prey or wild beasts wistfully watching one another; casting fearful and defying looks, previously to pouncing upon and mutually devouring each other. The question

is, who shall have power, wealth, glory ? There is
no room left for justice. The one idea is aggran-
disement and conquest by diplomatic ruse or brute
force. Alliances are concluded, the assertion being
loud and wide that universal peace is the sole object
in view; yet he who contracts those alliances has
spent his life in unsheathing the sword and creating
a vast empire by dint of cannon.

I do not wish my country to become the accom-
plice of such; I would rather see it isolated, seeking
indissoluble alliances only in conformity with justice.
What matter to us if Germany and her Chancellor
plan fresh conspiracies ? that nation is truly great
whose history is free from blot. If in the future
some great international iniquity were about to be
carried through, the French nation alone would still
find in itself enough of courage and virtue to place
its might in the service of right, for my country belongs to the proud race of knights of the crusades.
Glory may at times intoxicate and mislead her, but
she soon recovers from her illusions, preferring honour
and justice to mere glory, choosing rather to fall with
justice than to succeed without !

In the struggle for supremacy, victory will always
favour the clear-sighted; but it is important that
intelligence should walk hand in hand with honesty
and generosity.

III.

THE barrack, the school—such are, to the eyes of the
observer, the characteristic features of contemporary
Germany.

The Germans worship physical strength and intellect. Nowhere else does military power stand
on more solid bases, or is science more universally
cultivated.

Look at Berlin : soldiers everywhere ! In France,
the uniform is almost concealed; in Germany, a show
is made of it. Irksome to us ; a kind of stiff pride
to them. How gorgeous a barrack is the capital of
the new empire !

Every morning, except on holidays, regiments, on
their way to Tempelhof, the manœuvring grounds,

march, preceded by their bands, through the main
thoroughfares. Before starting they call at the imperial palace, there to take their colours. On their
return they replace them therein. The palace is
indeed the store-room of colours. When the standard-
bearers enter its gates, the drums beat in accompani-
ment to the shrill notes of the fifers and the strains
of the whole bands.

The old Emperor, standing at his window, nods
a salute to his beloved army. He seems to be the
first soldier of his people. What of the palace ? . . .
Does not that simple square edifice, with its four
eagles—one at each of the four corners of its roof,—
and its four pillars at its front entrance, remind us
of an imperial military guard-room ?

Barracks, chiefly in those States which grouped
themselves around Prussia to form the new empire,
are of recent construction. They may be seen, as
it were, in full bloom in Bavaria, in Würtemberg,
in Hanover, in Saxony : size, elegance, and strength,
regardless of cost. There they confront us almost
proudly, as the living proof of a military organisation unsurpassed and even unattained in any country,
at any time, at any stage of human civilisation. I
often wondered whence that nation, said to be so
poor, obtained the means for building *palaces* for its
two million soldiers.

It is not solely to gratify their natural admiration for brute force that Germans thus organise and extend their military power : they obey the dictates of a practical necessity. The history of the past centuries has taught them that their danger is always from the West.

The phantoms of Louis XIV. and of Napoleon I. are always terrible to the German eye. Germans are well aware that beyond the Rhine, between the ocean and that fatal stream, powerful weapons may be raised. When, in the midst of the last war, in his famous journey to European Courts, Thiers, at Vienna, inquired from L. de Ranke, " What is then the aim of Germany? " the old historian replied, " To destroy the work of Louis XIV." To-day, if questioned on their object, the regulators of the imperial policy might, if they frankly spoke their mind, say, " Our aim is to keep in readiness for the Louis XIV. or Napoleon of the future."

What they would not disclose is the fearful meaning they attach to their being in readiness. So long as France is France will the Germans be uneasy. An instinctive fear pervades their minds whenever they cast their eyes towards the Rhine. Their unexpected, unheard-of victories seem to them more the outcome of a providential will than the result of bravery, of long-prepared tactics and genius. The wise policy that hit upon the right moment to pounce upon and take unprepared France by surprise, did more towards ensuring success than the octogenarian warrior. The Germans, however, contrive to take a different view of their triumph, and to slumber peacefully, safely guarded by their great captain, and the watchful care of their great statesman.

Over and over again I experienced pleasure in suddenly disturbing their tranquillity. " What will you do," I inquired, " the day when Moltke and Bismarck have passed away ? " They shook their heads, and smilingly replied, " Moltke cannot die ; he has disciples. The army organised by his care will protect Germany against all emergencies." " But who is to succeed the Chancellor ? Has he, like Moltke, imparted his audacious genius to any disciple ? "

To that my interlocutors made no answer, and resumed their interrupted slumber.

Prince von Bismarck, unlike his countrymen, does not place implicit confidence in " Alexander's generals." His security does not lie so much in the strength of his Pomeranians as in the weakness of France. France powerful,—that means uncertainty, peril to the Chancellor's achievements ; it means an obstacle to Prussia in her work of violence, ruse, and dogged cunning. I say Prussia and not Germany; for Prussians are unlike all other Germans, whether

Bavarians, Saxons, Würtembergers, Hanoverians, or Rhinelanders.

To-day the whole of Germany revolves in the orbit marked out by Prussia; the idea of German unity binds closely together in the same ambition and interest all the States of the Empire; the French, in the eyes of any German, are still the enemy, yet the Germans are particularists. Their political unity is not the spontaneous result of the normal evolution of their national genius, it came from without: the Confederate States were, as we might say, blended and kneaded together with the blood of France, and by the skilful and ruthless hand of Prussia. They are aware of it, and are convinced that a defeat might destroy that which a victory created. A successful military blow from France would suffice to destroy that unity: such is the emergency to be prevented or guarded against at any cost.

That fear is the mainspring of the Chancellor's foreign policy. To have vanquished unprepared France was not enough; she must be mutilated. To have mutilated her was not sufficient; she must be rendered powerless, isolated, or artfully embroiled in distant adventures, until she could safely be, so to speak, quartered and annihilated as a nation.

My country will, I trust, see through such schemes and thwart their execution. The overgrown ambi-

tions of a national policy, wielded even by an iron
hand, and the coalitions of powerful empires, must
never succeed against a nation like France. Her
vitality is such that twenty revolutions have not
exhausted her; divided into innumerable factions,
the prey to intestine dissensions, she nevertheless still
retains the first place among nations, she disturbs and
causes apprehension to her foes; and mindful, above
all, of social and humanitarian progress, she, amidst
a thousand obstacles, opens to others the road to
the future.

If the destiny of France were, to become the
great peacemaker of the modern world; if, seeing
the mistake of military vanity, the folly of conquest,
she were to devote her renewed genius to the generous development of science, to the fraternity and political freedom of nations,—Germany would not even
then sheathe her sword again. So long as the Empire continues will Germany suffer from the effects of
its origin. Brought into life by brute force, through
that alone she is doomed to subsist. Her fortresses
may then be moved: they may watch the East instead of the West; but the ever-growing Panslav-
ism of the East will again impose on Germany the
overwhelming necessity of keeping up her military
power.

However superficially one may have observed the

race-antipathy between Germans and Slavs, one can but foresee an imminent shock between Russia and Germany. Wisdom and political skill, and the family ties of sovereigns, may delay the outbreak; but sooner or later will national passions burst forth. Nations, like races, are exposed to certain fatalities: who knows if, some day appointed by Providence, an irresistible necessity may not urge Germany to seek France, not for contest, but to buy with indispensable restitutions, an alliance become, for her, a question of life or death?

It is not within my province to discuss military matters. I am in no way competent to deal with that subject, being one of those whose dearest wish is to *transform swords into scythes and spears into ploughshares.* At the same time, I beg to venture a moral thought suggested to me by reflecting on German militarism. We at home seem to know it but very little. We see in it but an organised piece of machinery, and we forget the invisible soul, the moral spring, that sets in motion that formidable machine.

With its discipline and hierarchy, the German army is but the expression of the general spirit of the people,—a spirit of respect and passive obedience.

The German race has preserved that which we unfortunately have lost. It does not criticise; it simply and passively obeys. The *commando,* as they

have it, is always and everywhere heeded. It is, no
doubt, uttered by intelligent guides, and the recipi-
ents never discuss its merits. That phenomenon,
is to be met with alike in politics as in teaching,
in business as in the army, in public life as in home
circles.

Question the Germans themselves : you will soon
ascertain what they take pride in. Certainly not in
their climate : they all dream of an Italian sky. Nor
indeed in their soil : they all talk about the soil of
France, its fertility and products. They do not boast
of their wealth: their multitudes emigrate to America,
there to realise fortunes. Their marvellous fecundity
itself is to them no cause of pride. . . . Their great
boast is their army and their universities.

Chauvinism has crossed the Rhine. It rules there
as a master. No German is to be found who does
not consider his nation invincible by the number and
worth of its soldiers, the ability of its chiefs, the
superiority of its organisation and of its armaments.
But the learned there—and they are numerous—
above all extol and glorify their schools, which they
proclaim to be unrivalled. One of the most famous
German professors expressed the opinion of all his
colleagues throughout the empire in a brilliant but
rather exaggerated panegyric, which a foreigner would
not read without serious and legitimate reserve, per-

haps not even without his feelings being ruffled at the assertions therein contained.[1]

The author feels amazed that, in the thirteenth century, when France alone enjoyed the privilege of being the school of the *civilised* world, " no one in Germany foresaw how important it was for the empire, if it wished to lay the foundation of its power, and to create national unity, to possess its imperial school " (p. 7).

Although Germany was the last country in which universities were introduced and developed, she " has to-day become their land of predilection ; and such is the extension and the perfection of the scientific skill they have reached, that they are to-day without equal in the world, and alone worthy of their great name " (p. 28).

" It is in the universities that the individuality of German genius finds its most perfect expression and satisfaction for its noblest aspirations. The university is an integral part of the intellectual genius of Germany ; and wherever German activity appears, there appears also some imitation of her high schools " (p. 35).

" To universities must be ascribed the broad views of German intellect. They moulded German nature

[1] Die Universitäten, Sonst und Jest, von Dr Joh. Jos. Tegu. von Döllinger : München, 1871.

into the most strongly *universalist* type ; for in that nature is to be found, in a greater variety and more plentifully than in any other cultivated nation, true *humanitarianism*, true *cosmopolitanism.* [7]

It would be difficult to meet with any other national writer speaking with such praise of the intellectual organisation of his own country. However, all impartial minds are bound to acknowledge, in a measure, the truth of some of those assertions.

IV.

THE TEMPERAMENT OF NATIONS—NATIONAL GENIUS—INDELIBIL-
ITY OF RACES—DUALITY OF THE GERMAN BRAIN : SCHEMING
AND DREAMING ; POSITIVIST AND ACTIVE—THE ITALIAN
BRAIN, PRACTICAL AND DIPLOMATIC ; THE FRENCH, RATIONAL
AND IMPULSIVE ; THE GERMAN, BICEPHALIC—INFLUENCE OF
BRAIN-DUALITY UPON THE HISTORY OF GERMANY.

THE institutions, the activity, and the future of a
nation depend chiefly upon its temperament, its character, and genius. Knowledge of these qualities, however, is doubtless insufficient to form an adequate appreciation ; it is necessary also to take into account
the various circumstances, the secret inspirations, that
determine action, as also what may be called the age
of such nation. These data, nevertheless, may be
considered as indicating the paramount factor. We
modern nations, in our studies of retrospective history, do not understand the nations that preceded
us, unless we succeed in unveiling their national
soul ; then indeed, and only then, can we succeed in
bringing past generations to life again.

For, indeed, how can we explain those colossal absolute monarchies of the East—of India, Persia, Egypt—if we lose sight of the submissiveness of such ancient nations, moving, like so many flocks of sheep, according to the mighty will of the theocratic heroes whom, in those distant times, public opinion looked upon, with dismal veneration, as being the very incarnation of human majesty and divine authority? Could we ever understand Rome, her conquests and world-wide rule, if we did not bear in mind the boundless ambition both of its founders and of its people, their steadfastness of purpose, their powerful organisation, as also that proud faith in their mission which expressed itself in the famous maxim, " Parcere subjectis et debellare superbos "? Consider the nations that have passed away: the explanation of their destiny is always found in their national genius.

With even still more truth does that law apply to contemporary nations.

To the political and diplomatic aptitude of Prussia must be ascribed all her aggrandisements; the chivalrous and ardent spirit of France prompts her always to join and help any great and just cause, heedless of her own interest. Never, indeed, could the national ambition which gradually laid hold of Prussia, and transformed that small cramped State

into the leading kingdom of the old German confederation, have developed itself out of the quiet and
meek temperament of the southern German.

It is not German blood alone that flows through
the veins of the inhabitants of the shores of the
Northern Ocean and Brandenburg. Those broad
faces, those square skulls, that complexion, in most
cases brown, that proverbial osseousness (*ossature*),
remind us of another blood,—that of the Tartar
hordes of yore. However, without retracing the
origin of such races, without going too far back
in our historical investigations, without even turning
towards that Germany so attractively depicted by
Madame de Staël, and considering Germans only as
we now see them, they offer numerous characteristic
features which enable us sufficiently to understand
the mighty nation that has so suddenly risen in
Central Europe.

The fusion of modern nations, the frequency of
their intercourse, the uniformity of their moral, intellectual, and Christian culture, may have narrowed
the wide gulf between them—they have not removed
it. Races are intermixed by means of alliances,
their fusion is cemented by mutual bloodshed, but
they preserve a distinction as marked as the languages they speak. The Slav remains Slav—the German, German—the Latin, Latin ; and even under the

pressure of the same centralised administration, sub-
jecting all individuals to the same routine, despite
the closest political unity, in a country like ours
may still be traced the various races we meet with—
the Celt, the Gaul, the Ligurian, the Norman, the
Roman. The variety of types has been preserved
almost entire.

Of modern nations I know few whose study could
be, for a Frenchman, of greater interest and higher
import than Germany.

For the better understanding of our qualities,
already too well known by us, as also for that of
our defects, which we too often forget, and also too
easily excuse, it is important that we should see our
own image drawn in relief, *chased*, on a German
" background." Man is so constituted that with him
appreciation is the result of comparison, and is in
proportion to the contrast between the objects compared, whose features are more boldly brought out
in opposition. He who never saw the endless and
monotonous plain, where, from the midst of the
vegetation, rises the blazing and radiant sun, cannot
appreciate the mountain.

The better I knew Germany, the better also I
understood France, and the more I loved her.

The study of German genius, if we consider only
its great philosophers and divines, its critics and

historians, its writers and poets, does not afford a clear conception of one of the most salient features of that nation. I mean a fundamental fact that everywhere in Germany is too conspicuous to be passed over — the constant contradiction between theory and its application, speculation and reality, pure reason and practical reason.

The German is a dreamer fanciful and immense ; but with positive wisdom, he is ever mindful of his interests. His lucubrations and his dreams idealise, with boundless audacity, all they dwell upon ; but in the management of his affairs he only follows the ordinary common - sense of real life. When one reads his idealist poets, one fancies the German, with his blue eyes always raised towards his dull grey sky, in search of stars. What a mistake! those eyes are cast on the ground in search of the best path to pursue.

He passionately sings Schiller's great hymn to bliss—

> " Clasp each other, innumerable phalanxes,
>   In the universal embrace !
>   Brothers, above the starry dome,
>   A beloved Father must indeed dwell." [1]

Yet is there no people more particular, more careful of its own interests, less inclined to sacrifice itself

---

[1] 'An die Freude,' Schiller's Werke, Band I.

in a policy of sentiment for the brotherhood of man.

A clever politician, and with a more refined practical sense, the Italian never wanders in abstract theories. He delights in formulating his scientific conduct, he studies the philosophy of law, and writes, through the pen of his Machiavel, the famous chapters of " The Prince."

No less than the German does the Frenchman incline towards systems ; but the latter's ideas always clear, his deductions always precise, preserve him from the wanderings of transcendental idealism and too vulgar materialism. His natural love of clearness keeps him away from problems that present no possible solution. In fact, when his brain has got hold of a theory, whether it relate to religion, morality, politics, or business, some sort of honesty urges him on, and leaves him no peace until he has made up his mind, often in spite of the resistance of reality, to reduce it into a tangible practicality. That is the chief source of our greatness and of our failings. If speculative ideas, which rule opinion on religious, moral, or political questions, be correct and just, then the impulse they give our fiery temperament carry us to the highest summits. Are they wrong? We no longer hover in high regions, we are lowered, and we obstinately persist in crawling, seeking, even in our

failure and our mishaps, some kind of food for our
fatal logic.

Instead of mistrusting the idea that leads him, the
Frenchman rebels against the facts that are opposed
to him. Instead of condemning the inefficiency of
his theories, he accuses all that prevents their reali-
sation. He denounces, excommunicates, upsets, de-
stroys; until at last, bloody reality giving him the
lie, he acknowledges the fatal spell of preconceived
ideas.

The Frenchman has a brain wherein the idea
catches fire and expresses itself at once by an action,
but the German is a sort of *bicephalic* being.

The latter presents sometimes Kant's mighty and
meditative forehead, wherein the faculties of causality
are developed to the extreme; Goethe's olympian
features, full of grand poetical aspirations; sometimes
a broad skull with expanded temporals and an enor-
mous occipital predominance, sure signs of energetic
though unrefined instincts ruled over by a sort of
common-sense. The German thinks and schemes
with one brain; he conducts himself and acts, as it
were, with another. It is not without interest that
we observe that Kant, whose genius left such a lasting influence upon the spirit of the German people
and its philosophical education, dogmatically consecrated the distinction, the separation, the contradic-

tion even between the ideal speculative world over
which rules pure reason alone, and which, according
to that philosopher, teaches us indeed nothing of
absolute reality, and the real world of action, wherein
practical reason must act, subdued by God Himself,
by duty, by conscience.

The dualism we notice in the physiognomical
appearance of the German, as well as in his metaphysics, is also obvious in the leading facts of his
national life—in his religion, his politics, and his
history.

Protestant Germany laid down the principle of
the supreme authority of the Scriptures, rejecting all
papal domination. As a matter of fact, she obeys
less the Bible than synods and consistories, which
create an orthodoxy, and whose ruling decisions are to
her quite as binding as papal dictates for Roman
Catholics. Theoretically, Germany maintains the
great unity of which every German is passionately
fond ; practically, she remains the most particularist
of nations, most attached to her local administration, to her provincialism—the most decentralised
of nations, not only in Europe, but in the whole
world. Theoretically, Germany has laid down the
most radical of doctrines as regards national and
humanitarian progress ; practically, there is no nation,
not excepting England, which has more carefully

preserved ancient customs, and which remains more faithful to the traditions of the past. As in the fifteenth century, everywhere are still to be seen houses with pinion roofs and cornices in carved wood, high belfries wherein the night-watcher calls out the hours as they wear on, and shouts " Fire !" in case of conflagration ; ancient corporations and universities, as in the middle ages.

All that was hatched in the metaphysical and idealistic mind of Germans, for the last century, does not bear fruit in Germany. The idea, like a seed, seems to possess but latent life with that people ; and it is on French soil that it thrives and that its ripe fruit is often gathered.

The sceptical idealism of a Kant created, with us, legions of scholars sceptical in facts ; the purely dogmatical irreligion from beyond the Rhine often became the generating principle of the practical irreligion of the Frenchman.

A superficial observer might feel disposed to denounce as duplicity and falseness that intellectual dualism of German genius. Frenchmen, above all, will hardly understand how a mind, theoretically convinced, does not strictly look upon its conviction as being the inflexible absolute rule of its life and of its actions.

If we reflect well, we perceive, on the contrary,

in the fundamental distinction between the speculative world and the world of action, a grand philosophical and moral truth, and, for man, a guarantee
of wisdom. Nothing more true than the inefficiency
of our human systems,—nothing wiser than to doubt
the complete truth of our individual views, always
so narrow. Reserve and circumspection well become genius ; and whatever the audacity of its
flight, reality leaves it far behind, constantly chal-
lenging it. There are always more things in heaven
and on this earth, and even *between* earth and
heaven, to speak like Hamlet, than our philosophy
ever dreamt of.

The mighty men who stir the world, create nations,
lay the foundations of or reform religions, never build
ready-made systems in philosophy, in religion, or in
politics ; they set to work the natural and divine
forces in which they put their faith, satisfied to
discern the facts with superior perspicacity, and to
serve with all their genius the panting interests of
their country or of mankind.

To that characteristic constitution of the German
brain must, I believe, be ascribed the undeniable
broadness of its views, and the extension—I would
almost say the span—of its mind.

German views are broad but confused ; ours are
clear and correct. Their stumbling-block is vague-

ness, obscurity; we must fear being too superficial. They are diffuse and prolix; we can be brief and concise. They heap facts together; we penetrate the law that rules them. Patient like the ox that, with indefatigable muscles, slowly ploughs the field, they prepare the ground for the sower. They excel in digging and unearthing documents; they could have brought to life all the hieroglyphics of ancient Egypt. It is hard to decide whether they could ever have produced a Champollion. German genius is the result of long patience: it searches, it investigates, it organises; it creates not. The marvellous success of its arms furnishes the proof of this. In astronomy, it was anticipated by an Italian—Galileo; in experimental science, by an Englishman—Newton; in modern philosophy, by a Frenchman—Descartes. But in works, the achievement of which requires tenacity and impartiality, qualities resulting from a certain broadness of views, the Germans excel. Their productions relating to criticism and history are noticeable by the abundance of documents, and profound erudition. As for the great movement which, in our days, leads all scientific men to the origin of species and the long-unknown world of the microbes, wherein medicine will perhaps discover the secret of the most fearful diseases that afflict mankind,—was it, I ask, Germany that gave the

impulsion? No: it was England; and, above all,
France.[1]

As regards the glory of having obtained from the
human lyre the most powerful, the deepest, the most
delightful and divine sounds, the entire honour
belongs to Germany. In German genius harmony
found its immortal interpreters.

The names of Beethoven and Mozart are indeed
unrivalled. The greatest dreamers belong to that
German race, so positivist, so realistic in many cases.
Those heavy-looking people are at heart, under their
coarse exteriors, truly and marvellously poetical; they
delight in the shadow of the forests, in the sonorous
voices of the pines under their misty skies; and the
most inveterate beer-drinker stops as bewitched before
his foaming tankard, when he hears the bow striking
a prelude from Bach, or a symphony from Beethoven.

Music has no expanding influence upon the German, but concentrates his emotions. Look at him
when under the spell; he does not keep his head
erect, he drops it; there is no flash of light in his
eyes, he stares or shuts them. Motionless, impassive,
he forgets the outside world, and seems attentively to
listen to that divine voice, the echoes of which German music excels in awaking.

[1] See Appendix G.

V.

MORAL CHARACTER OF THE GERMAN—HIS COMPLEXITY—HIS
PERSEVERANCE — FRANKNESS AND RESERVE — SPIRIT OF
DISCIPLINE—CALM AND ORDERLY EVEN IN HIS EXCESSES—
SCENE FROM A STUDENTS' BANQUET—RESPECT OF HIER-
ARCHY—LOVE OF THE USE OF TITLES IN CIVIL LIFE—
INDEPENDENCE.

THE moral character of the German is no less intricate than his mind. I will only mention a few
instances of it, from among the most peculiar, con-
trasting most with our national habits.

I often wondered at the precocious gravity and
diligence of German children. They seem to be
born disciplined and obedient, as others are born
insubordinate and fickle. Their first education, at
home, still develops those native qualities; it has,
indeed, no trouble to succeed; for those square little
heads, whose quiet, almost apathetic blood is so
different from our fiery and excitable natures, are
truly better shaped for obedience than for initiative.
Violence, brutality even, tames and reduces them; it
would revolt and exasperate us.

C

The German is more governable than many other nations ; he more easily submits to the yoke. Nothing in him of the exuberance of those races over which the sun shines radiantly without exhausting them. The well-known proverb, *in vino veritas*, does not apply to those whom beer never causes to lose self-control. The Germans, it may be, owe some of their qualities to their national drink.

Now that science better knows the organic conditions of passion, of sensibility, of thought even, we may with reason often seek in infinitesimal things the cause of phenomena of a superior order. Who knows, that a little less alcohol in the veins of the French people might not suffice to appease the effervescence of its blood and moderate its indiscipline ? The German has no cause to fear our nervous excitement ; his temperament leads him to be patient, laborious, and submissive. The fatality of his *régime*, far from destroying those dispositions, confirms them. Excesses themselves do not disturb the equilibrium of those massive natures. " We see our Germans," says Montaigne, " drowned in wine, recollect their lodgings, the pass-word, and their rank." [1]

That is, no doubt, the cause of the perseverance and of the proverbial obstinacy of the German. In all he undertakes he shows those qualities ; in busi-

[1] Essays, book ii. chap. ii.

ness pursuits, as in the carrying out of an idea; in his scientific undertakings, as in his politics; in his individual productions, as in his national wishes. It is Strauss with his mythical idea, Schopenhauer with his pessimism, Bismarck with his pan-Germanism.

The French are impatient and impulsive; the Germans imperturbably calm: they know how to wait. An obstacle discourages the former; the latter tire the obstacle. The one cuts the gordian knot; the other might succeed in untying it. The one is a spark that might set the world ablaze; the other a mass that might crush it.

If vivacity of temperament imparts frankness, heaviness produces reserve. It is easy to see through a warm nature that abandons itself; it is not so easy to penetrate the innermost recesses of a calm nature which a deep feeling does not move beyond ordinary limits. Those fair heads and blue eyes are far from being candid and transparent; and simple indeed one would be not to notice, in intercourse with them, much more than the phrases, polite but devoid of refinement, that fall from German lips. One fault of Frenchmen is, too great an excess of frankness; of the Germans, reserve to excess. We speak too much, they too little; we are eloquent, they taciturn; deceit is the exception with us, with them the exception is frankness. The vivacity and

suppleness of our language permit of our saying anything ; when the German speaks on certain topics,
though with a masterly command over his tongue, he
can scarcely avoid coarseness and brutality.

The French, quick to criticise, will hardly comprehend the spirit of respect, the habit of discipline,
and the power of hierarchy with the German people.
To appreciate that phenomenon, one must have lived
in the country, mixing with the population in its
everyday life—not merely have seen Prussian regiments marching through *Unter den Linden.* Nothing
superficial in that phenomenon ; it is not the result
of brutal authority and of servile fear ; it is not
isolated and to be met with only in military life ;
it is universal. It exists even where authority is
only the result of the free agreement of all those
who elected it, in *fêtes* and joyful meetings, where
discipline seems out of place. Of this I will give
an instance, the significance of which is all the more
striking, as the circumstances were such as authority
would seem powerless in and discipline entirely at
the mercy of revelry.

German students are grouped in free associations
—*Burschenschaft, Corps, Landsmannschaft,* and various
other corporations. Such associations, entirely foreign
to politics, have, as we shall see,[1] no other object than

[1] See chapter xii.

to bring more closely together the vast numbers of students. As the result of German particularism and of ancient traditions, their sole aim is simply fellowship in the worship of honour, of religion, of freedom, and of the German fatherland, or else of mental association in the study of the same science. Small republics of mirthful though sometimes quarrelsome dispositions, they administer themselves, elect their leader, and form small states within the great university confederation. Their members meet weekly in a private room named the *Kneipe*, and there, in a meeting which they call their *Commers*, discuss the business of the association.

I was never more forcibly struck than by the behaviour of those youths, and the spirit of discipline that pervades even those joyful revels where beer flows recklessly.

The chairman is seated at the head of a long table, round which are seated members and visitors alike. Before him is a rapier (*Schläger*). Striking the table with that, he obtains silence, and gives his orders. National hymns and joyous strains follow in turn at the chairman's *commando ;* the long toasts are drunk in cadence, according to directions given with the sword. When the meeting is prolonged, the chairman yields his seat to the youngest of members, who thus becomes *Regent ·* during the last and gayest

hours. The Regent, with frail authority, wields the
sceptre, allowing all a certain freedom, at which he,
as the youngest member, cannot rightly take offence.
The ties of discipline are loosened, but not severed.
There I again met with the same spirit of respect
and submission that rules soldiers, and could not
help thinking that such virtue must indeed have
deep roots in the customs of the people to permit
of its being respected by the exuberant mirth of
excited youth, and of its ruling even the frothy beer.

One of the popular signs of that respect for
hierarchy is the carefulness with which, in the
intercourse of civil life, Germans at home address
one another by their respective titles.

The subtleness of etiquette even distinguishes the
teacher (*Lehrer*) from the doctor (*Doctor*) and the
professor (*Professor*) lecturing in a university. Such
is not the case in Italy, a land essentially authorita-
tive, where hierarchy was in some way consecrated,
where the science of law, that is, of government,
reached its highest achievement, and where the
teacher (*Maestro*) conquered the first place, even in
the opinion of the masses. But in Italy the regard
entertained for the teacher only reflects that enjoyed
by sacerdotal hierarchy ; in Germany, it is the
counterpart of that enjoyed by universities. Never-

theless it would be a great mistake to conceive the German, so disciplined, sometimes servile, as incapable of independence and liberty.

There is now passing in Germany something which deserves not only to be noticed, but to be pondered well —the political struggle between the Chancellor and the Parliament on the score of home reforms. The unbending will of the master wants to control the opinion of the deputies. He knocks repeatedly at the door of the Reichstag. What is the answer of the representatives of the country? Do they bow before the power of the despot?—do they abdicate their privileges and rights before his iron will? To hear superficial observers, who, to flatter our national vanity, are pleased to extol our independence, our liberalism, and deprecate constantly the mechanical, automatic militarism of Germany, such might be the conclusion. It is an error. The practical sense of his interests protects the German not only against the eloquence of a tribune, but against the State reasons alleged by all despots.

Discipline is the school of liberty. Obedience and submission are not servility. To give way to arbitrary whims—that is servitude; to bow before the law and the authority that enacts it—such is the honour of being free. The greatest numbers of slaves

are recruited from the ranks of those who pride themselves most in their independence, in rebellion even,
just as simple believers and superstitious people are
found amongst such as are without conviction and
without faith.

VI.

PUBLIC INSTRUCTION AND MODERN CIVILISATION—THE GREATEST
NATION THAT WHERE THE ORGAN OF PUBLIC INSTRUCTION
MOST PERFECT—THIS SEEN IN GERMANY—THE THREE
DEGREES OF PUBLIC INSTRUCTION—SUPERIORITY OF THE
MODERN WORLD OVER THE MIDDLE AGES AND ANTIQUITY—
PRIMARY EDUCATION—SUPERIORITY OF GERMANY—RELIGION
NOT REPUDIATED BY HER—RELIGIOUS INSTRUCTION OBLIGA-
TORY FOR CHILDREN—SPREAD OF ELEMENTARY TUITION
UNDER THE INFLUENCE OF CHRISTIANITY AND DEMOCRACY
—RELIGION A NECESSARY PHASE FOR THE EVOLUTION OF
THE HUMAN SPECIES AND OF INDIVIDUALS.

THE most necessary element in a civilised nation is
public instruction, as institutions meant to promote
the acquisition and lasting development of general
culture are to her the chief vital organ. Intellectual
superiority eventually gives a nation predominance
over her neighbours; for if virtues raise us in the
eyes of God, science makes us higher in those of
men. Military power itself is only the result of a
more advanced stage in science. It is science that
builds fortresses scarcely protruding above ground,
that turns out ironclads, grinds the best swords,

devises the means of mowing down the greatest number of human beings, invents the art of killing wholesale, and changes man, in the hour of struggle, into the most bloodthirsty of carnivorous animals, if justice does not control the violence and wrath of his instincts. It is science which forges for the nations more terrible weapons, offensive and defensive, the use of which, though she did not create them, conscience can and must decide.

These thoughts rush into one's mind when treading German soil, and seeing at each step the military show which the Empire delights in. The wild beast is quiet enough to-day; but, though resting, she watches recumbent, sharpening constantly both teeth and claws, her eyes fixed on the horizon,—now towards the East, now in the direction of the West —chiefly there !

The ambition of domination might alone suffice to explain the universal ardour provoked by science everywhere in the modern world. The question is less to know the universe than to learn to master it. The aim in view is not so much the satisfaction of the performance of a duty as the intoxicating hope of commanding all forces, the free and intelligent as the brutal and unconscious.

However, there is, methinks, more nobleness in such despotic views than in the sectarian plans of those who constantly oppose science to religion, and desire the organisation of science only the better to secularise a people, as, with a new euphemism, say the false priests of a humanity without faith, without a Mediator, and without a God. Violent spirits can be calmed down, those whom strength and power intoxicate can also be appeased; but what can be expected from minds stamped with scepticism, incapable of loving truth and of lifting their eyes above this earth?

Germany, proud of her strength, offers in her national life no phenomenon of senility. Her vices are rather those of barbarism than of decrepitude. She presents a peculiar mixture of primitive rudeness and civilisation. Her barbarous and uncouth nature proceeds from her blood itself; her civilised and superior qualities from her education.

My object in closely studying Germany is not to depict her vices, in order to be agreeable to my countrymen, and to purposely lessen their most redoubtable adversary; on the contrary, I endeavour to examine, with a calm and impartial mind, the elements of Germany's strength and vitality for the information of my country, and to guard her against all illusions. The secret of victory for a manly people does not lie in lowering his adversary but in studying him, and, once knowing him, to struggle relentlessly in order to surpass him.

A glance over the civilised world and its intellectual culture suffices to ascertain the constant division of public instruction into three degrees— primary, secondary, and superior education.

Primary education is, or nearly so, everywhere identical; it applies to the masses—to all, without distinction: its object is to teach the child how to read, write, and calculate. Reading, writing, and arithmetic—such are, with modern as with ancient nations, the A B C of intellectual culture. In that light the modern world may, however, claim incontestable superiority over both the middle ages and antiquity. Some centuries back a few privileged men had alone the opportunity of learning. Intoxicated with power, and satisfied with their life of constant warfare, most lords and nobles glorified in knowing nothing, not even to sign their own names except with the sword. Others shared with priests and wealthy people the privilege of being educated. Nowadays, in our societies eager for knowledge, all are bent on learning — all may and must learn. Wilful ignorance has become an offence against the law, and almost all modern States regard primary education as a civic duty. The first place is for those who display the greatest craving for learning, and whose rulers display the keenest tact and most practical intellect in satisfying that craving, without infringing on the supreme rights of conscience and family influence.

The diffusion of elementary knowledge providentially secures the full ripening of a larger number of intellects—sacred germs sown by God Himself in the human family, and which often are not brought to light, because the selfishness of castes, or some other social fatality, deprives them of the first conditions of growth. Who can say how many of such obscure germs have never arrived at maturity, having been crushed and smothered in barren furrows! They only asked for a ray of light, in order to develop themselves and thrive. Those who could have made the sun shine over them left them in darkness. The worst is, that there were politicians to justify such a system, and look upon the ignorance of the masses—that *Malthusianism* of the mind—as being a sort of guarantee for public order and social prosperity! No doubt, in education dangers lie hidden ; but where in this world is the good without danger? Those who become frightened and who draw back are the pusillanimous. According to them we should suppress life, since it entails suffering and death. Inundations and fires are no rare occurrences. Did ever any one, asks M. de Maistre, propose doing away with water and fire?

It will not be the least honour of Christianity to

have brought to life a new world wherein truth and liberty must some day become the ruling passions; wherein also the first duty of charity must have been the universal diffusion of truth, and the wielding of its first tools by the poorest and most obscure of men.

If we travel through Germany from north to south, from the Rhine to the Elbe, and witness the ardour with which the people frequent the various schools, as also the special care with which the divers Governments contrive to meet that impulse and conform to popular wishes in that direction, it is impossible for us to misunderstand the vitality of popular instruction.

The schools are scattered all over the country. The smallest village possesses its palace: it is the *Volksschule.*

That diffusion of elementary knowledge with the various modern nations has had, until now, two causes — the Christian and the democratic spirit. Under the influence of the former, Germany, for the last three centuries, has everywhere created popular schools. The Bible being the oracle of all that believed, it was indeed indispensable that all should learn how to read. Under the impulse of the latter, France has rather enlarged the limits of popular instruction ; for Frenchmen, being all destined some day to become electors, it was also indispensable that

they should be able to read. Under the double
impulse of the Christian and the democratic spirit,
the United States themselves have also given popular
instruction a wonderful impetus.

But while Germany had the wisdom to give a
legitimate place in primary schools to religion and
its ministers, while she regarded religious instruction
taught by a minister of religion as being an element
not to be dispensed with, and that, in school programmes, should occupy the place of honour, France
could not resist irreligion. She closed the school
door against the priest and his catechism, as though,
when faithful to his mission, he were a suspicious
and dangerous being—as though religious doctrine
were a worthless teaching.

The vigilance of the parents, it was alleged, could
be depended upon to supply that which some amongst
them might regard as a deficiency. Nobody respects
more than I the liberty of parents ; but, at the same
time, who knows not the want of initiative, the inertia
of the masses in France ? and since the State could,
without trespass, impose upon parents the compulsory
primary education of their children, it would have
fulfilled a patriotic duty in imposing religion as one
essential branch of the programme. To require children to attend religious lectures contrary to their
parents' belief would have been an iniquity, a

tyranny; but to enact that they should be brought up in a belief in conformity with their parents' creed would have been the work of a strong and wise government.

The heads of families who, in France, live without any positive religion, belonging to no denomination, would no doubt have exclaimed against the alleged trespass on their liberty of conscience. An exception to the rule might have been made in their favour, for they are but a minority, and it is not for minorities that laws are enacted, although binding them like the rest. Indeed it is a fact, rather painful to acknowledge, that the greater number of such fathers are either bent on, or would easily submit to, seeing their children brought up devoid of faith and in the ignorance of God!

And what, in the soul of the child, will take the place of religion? If, as the positivists assert, religion were only a transitory form of humanity, applying to only one of the phases of its evolution, religious knowledge should still be kept up in schools.

The law that rules the individual in his particular evolution—the highest scientific authority teaches it —is, and must be, a reproduction only of that which rules the species. If, then, the species passes through a certain phase, the individual must also pass through it, or run the risk of ignoring one of the laws of life.

Well, then, history testifies to it, the human species, at the outset of its expansion through centuries, is essentially and universally religious; therefore, according to scientific data, the individual, at the beginning of his short existence, should be religious. Physiological law is but one of the various aspects of biological law; and as, in the transformations of living creatures, the suppression of one of the links leads fatally to physiological monstrosities, so in moral progress, vices—that is, moral monstrosities—inevitably result from the suppression of one of its phases.

But, though proudly proclaiming ourselves the faithful adepts of science, we seldom curb our narrow prejudices before her broad teachings. We cultivate science too often in order to oppose her to whatever hinders us, to whatever counteracts our vain systems, to what we are unable to comprehend. We refer to her to prove that man began by being but a living cell that must have passed through the various forms of life and animality, from the protozoan to the superior vertebrate, before reaching his definite form: but we refuse to learn from her that children must be not only educated, but *religiously* educated; that the essential laws of nature are immutable, inexorable, and that their violation, either by nations or by individuals, must sooner or later result in death.

D

2

What a change if, freed from our own subjection, we understood, I do not say how to use science, but how to serve her? Sectarian ideas are the greatest element of disturbance in our own country; our fatal mania of making a social and political application prevents our organising that modern world, so great by its elements of vitality. Splendid aspirations broke forth in our country : never at any time, under any sky, was there witnessed such an impulse towards the equality, the fraternity, and the enfranchisement of men. Why, then, should the spirit of deceit and hatred have sown darnel in a field that gave such expectations ? When will the comedy, which is being played under the mask of those sacred principles, come to an end ? The only and true way to honour those principles is to sacrifice our selfishness, for they are not the means, they are the aim of life ; we must not make use of them, but promote them. What greater satisfaction could be afforded to all true patriots than to see France at last giving shape and form to her grand dreams, and proudly displaying herself to her neighbours as the model of a new people with whom fraternity expresses itself by universal benevolence, equality by the unflinching reign of the law, and liberty by personal initiative and large tolerance ?

51

VII.

SECONDARY EDUCATION SINCE THE RENAISSANCE—ITS ESSENTIAL
OBJECT—HOW THE GERMANS UNDERSTOOD IT—GYMNASIUMS
AND *REAL* SCHOOLS—THE STUDY OF CLASSICAL LANGUAGES
IN GYMNASIUMS—PREDILECTION OF THE GERMANS FOR THE
FRENCH TONGUE—THEIR NEGLECT OF SLAVONIC LANGUAGES
—ALSATIANS AND POLES—THE REVENGE OF JUSTICE.

SECONDARY education has been, since the Renaissance,
one of the leading features in the organisation of
public instruction.

Since then it has constantly extended its province.
Its chief object is to provide youth with the knowledge that will fit it for higher education. It
comprises two indispensable elements—the knowledge of mathematics and natural sciences, and that
of dead and modern languages. Without the former,
how could we understand nature, weigh its forces,
penetrate the secret of its life, measure its immensity?
The knowledge of the latter enables us to fathom
religion, philosophy, the life, the customs, the very
soul of mankind, the history of nations whose civil-

isation has disappeared, as well as that of contemporary peoples.

Before the Renaissance, Latin was almost the only language in use with the learned. Preoccupied with himself, with his social, civil, or religious life, man only cast a childish glance on nature, naively confident in his theories, and obstinately seeking therefrom the secret of this great universe, instead of trying to obtain it, through careful observations, from the universe itself. Conversant with Latin, and the most elementary notions of geometry and arithmetic, young men entered universities as students of the *faculty of arts*, thence embracing the study of divinity, philosophy, jurisprudence, or medicine, which then comprised all the branches of higher education.

But as soon as the various tongues spoken by previous civilisations unveiled to inquisitive mankind their unknown masterpieces, and the impulse that urged men towards science became stronger, it was found necessary to acquaint youth with the various idioms, to impart to it the knowledge of Greek and Hebrew besides Latin, to teach it Sanscrit and Eastern languages, dead as well as modern tongues, to place in its hands all the implements of experimental sciences, to initiate it into higher mathematics, without which it is impossible to master astronomy, chemistry, physics, biology, or any other scientific knowledge of nature.

The Germans appear to me to have very practically understood the real aim of secondary education.

They have not, like ourselves, invented that fatal *bifurcation* that prematurely separates the two main *tools* of intellectual culture in the hands of adolescence—I mean, the science of languages and mathematics. They, by the side of *real* schools (*Realschulen*), wherein the scientific and professional element predominated, created the gymnasium (*Gymnasien*), wherein literary pursuits occupy the leading place ; but, as M. Michel Breal very truly remarks,[1] " the *real* school is not the antithesis of the gymnasium, it is a kind of mixed gymnasium. Although born from the practical and utilitarian spirit of the times, it at the same time remained æsthetic and scientific. History and literature therein still occupy an important place, at the same time leaving plenty of room for mathematics, natural history, physics, and chemistry. In the higher classes the *real* school is better adapted for scientific studies than the gymnasium, though still competing with the latter in the field of literary pursuits. The chief difference between the two establishments is that the pupils of the gymnasium, their studies once over, complete

[1] Excursions pédagogiques : Paris, 1882.

their education at the university, whereas most of
the others, on leaving the *Realschule*, at once enter on
the pursuits of life. Teaching at the *Realschule* must
be more varied, though in many respects not so deep
as that of the *Gymnasien.*"

These well-defined attributions of the two German
institutions upon which secondary education is based
have been clearly and officially set forth, in Prussia,
by a ministerial circular of the 6th of October 1859.[1]

In fact, *real* schools never truly succeeded in competing with gymnasiums : it is in these that higher
education recruits most and the best of its disciples.
In my opinion, that institution is, among similar
institutions, that which, in all Europe, answers best
the true requirements of secondary education. Without neglecting mathematics or the leading scientific
facts, its chief object is a solid philological instruction.

I do not know schools where languages are better
and more carefully cultivated. Hebrew, Greek, and
Latin are there considered as being the classical
ancient tongues, and taught as such. The study of
the rudiments of Hebrew initiates young men into
the knowledge really most useful for the comprehension of Semitic languages, as for that of the
Bible, which plays so considerable a part in the

---

[1] Lehrpläne für die höheren schulen, &c.: Berlin, 1882.

religious life of Protestantism and of any Christian
scholar. The study of Greek gives the key to that
Hellenic world whose attraction is so great for all
who love æsthetics, for there it is that the human
ideal revealed itself under its most exquisite forms.
There is no modern genius that does not acknowledge a master in artistic Greece among her poets,
her philosophers, her historians, her scholars, her
orators, or her writers. The study of the Latin
tongue unveils the Roman world, and all that civilisation of which Rome was the first mighty personification, and which, on her disappearing, she be-
queathed to the barbarians, to those new nations who
grew and throve under the sun of God and Christ on
the shores of the Mediterranean, and held, and hold
now, under the name of the Latin races, the largest
place in universal history.

The study of Hebrew is optional in German gymnasiums; but lectures are nevertheless given in that
branch of knowledge, which is not the case in any
of the secondary education establishments in other
European countries, or in America. All young men
who intend embracing holy orders, or becoming doctors in philosophy, attend assiduously the Hebraical
lectures, desirous of acquiring an element indispensable to their ulterior education.

The leading modern languages—French, English,

Italian, Spanish—are taught also in gymnasiums.
French is always compulsory; and of all foreign
languages it is that which Germans learn most
readily. They may rebel inwardly against the
supremacy of French genius; they may look down
from the height of their German barbarity upon
those whom they call the Latin races—their conduct
itself gives them the lie; for the eagerness with
which, when children, they learn our grammar, and,
when older, acquaint themselves with our masterpieces, proves beyond doubt our ascendancy and
superiority. One willingly looks up to those above,
as one also disdains stooping to those beneath. If
the Germans evince, even in their educational system,
such lively preoccupation concerning Latin peoples,
and France especially, be sure it is that they really
feel our worth; and if they care little about Russia
and Slavonic tongues, it is that they, wrongly perhaps,
fancy that no good is to be derived from such study.

The legions of German masters, merchants, *em-
ployés*, who invade the Slavonic borders, do not
trouble themselves much about Russian: they preserve intact their own tongue, their civilisation, and
their superiority; they remain Germans, and speak
German; and their devouring individuality tries to
absorb those whom they regard as an inferior nation.

They should nevertheless be watchful. The Slavs

have scarcely entered the movement of modern civilisation. No one can tell where the colossal infant,
about which the keen-sighted Napoleon felt rather
uneasy, will stop in its progress; nor can any one
foresee what might be the fate of Germany if some
day she found herself as in the jaws of some formidable vice between Latin nations whom she taunts
with being senile, and the Slavs whom she delights
in considering as uncouth barbarians! She might
then repent the crime of making the mutilation of
France a condition of peace and security for her
future, and thus preventing, by a policy of violent
annexation, the harmony of two great nations. The
Frenchmen of Alsace and the Slavs of Poland will
some day recover their race and nationality: works
of violence cannot endure. All who have lived by
conquest and annexation have died dismembered.
History does not present a single instance to the
contrary. The famous prophetic decree that disturbed Belshazzar's banquet is written from century
to century, and by the same hand, whenever a
similar policy, intoxicated by similar triumphs, abandons itself to like orgies, provoking the same ven-
geance. However remote may be such prospects,
from them a vanquished patriot can derive solid,
virile hopes; for justice will, sooner or later, obtain
its legitimate and sacred revenge.

VIII.

SECONDARY EDUCATION CONTINUED—ITS *PREPARATORY* CHARACTER WISELY PRESERVED IN GERMANY—LITERARY AND SCIENTIFIC PROVISIONS — THREE FRENCH PREJUDICES INJURIOUS TO SECONDARY EDUCATION : FALSE POSITIVISM, IRRELIGION, SPIRIT OF CRITICISM AND PRECOCIOUS CULTURE —ORIGIN OF THE LAST OF THESE PREJUDICES—ITS DISASTROUS CONSEQUENCES.

SECONDARY education, in gymnasiums and real schools throughout Germany, has a great merit : it has preserved intact its *preparatory* character. The pupil who, at the expiration of seven or eight years' studies, undergoes his final examination (*absolutorium*) is not held to have any knowledge, but simply to be ready for acquiring knowledge. The laureate proudly carries his insignia—a cap and a scarf, with the colours of the gymnasium or real school he has just left. No difference between him and the students, save his appearance,—his cheeks yet free from scars —he has not yet fought any duel,—by a kind of awkwardness that reminds one of recruits. In whatever esteem the examination of maturity may be held, it is not a patent of science, but a simple testimonial, implying fitness for knowledge. Science exists only in higher education, and for those who, their age and culture considered, are fit for initiation in philosophy.

Premature appeal to reason has many disadvantages. In its development, the mind, like the body, is subject to certain normal laws ; and if the child's brain cannot, without danger to its physical health, be brought into activity before a certain age, neither can the metaphysical and rational faculties of the mind be exercised too soon, without jeopardising mental hygiene. The higher branches of knowledge imply the independent use of abstract reason. The question is no longer belief in a teacher, but seeing with one's own eyes, and being struck with the same evidence. Not only have we to observe facts likely to leave an impression on our imagination, we must conceive the ideal and transcendental law. Such work is unsuited to youthful minds. They are not yet expected to produce ; they must only receive. Memory must be in full activity, discreetly enriched, but not overloaded : what it will have gathered will, later on, act on the volition, the imagination, the reason itself, and will then become the chosen aliment of the first efforts of personal genius. Thus albumen, in the egg, is meant to feed the germ up to the time when, strong enough to live by itself, it breaks the shell.

The study of dead and modern languages is better calculated than any other to meet the requirements of all the faculties of youth. Of such a study memory bears the burden ; the faculties of imitation and the natural curiosity of the mind are directly set to work, since the question at issue is to acquire information respecting the thoughts of men and people foreign to one's self, as well as the best manner of rendering such thoughts in one's own tongue. Even then personal reason is stimulated by salutary efforts, since it is obliged to grasp the idea hidden in some expression often quite alien to the mother tongue.

It is well, however, to call the growing reason to reality ; to teach it to consider, not merely words, but the things which they indicate ; to excite its youthful activity to easy endeavours, such as the means of perfecting the result obtained by the study of mathematics and the elementary notions of experimental sciences. But let us not forget that these teachings are, and can be, but a remote initiation to true knowledge ; it is because of its having disregarded that feature that secondary education in France is becoming more and more misleading.

Three prejudices exercise over it a most disastrous

influence. False positivism, injudiciously fond of experimental sciences, deprecates dead languages, and, considering Latin and Greek exercises as occupying precious time stolen from more practical studies, it deprives French youth of the necessary tools for acquiring a knowledge of the great periods of civilisation. Irreligion is always contriving to lessen the value of religious instruction, and at last has succeeded in striking it out of the programme. In fine, rationalism foolishly brings about a premature manifestation of the spirit of criticism, and ignoring the true law of human nature, pretends to teach youth to think by itself, before learning to think through the guidance of a master.

The vice of hasty formation of youth is not new in Latin races; its origin may be traced as far back as the sixteenth century, when, under the influence of indiscipline in the faculties of arts, *facultates artium*, the universities declined.

The Jesuits, in order to overcome the spirit of insubordination, resorted to the celebrated system of "internat,"—that is, lodging and boarding of the pupils,—a system which soon became almost exclusive. The universities in France followed in the movement, even exaggerating its application, and depriving it of all moral or religious counterpoise. They even went farther: not satisfied with imprisoning between high

walls, under the vigilant and fatherly care of skilful
masters, a youth whose exuberance inspired fears,
that colleges might give a complete course of education to and return to society men ready to begin life,
they prematurely taught their pupils that which the
pupils should have learnt only in the universities.
They wanted youths to be *men* at the end of their
classical studies. As the field of knowledge grew
broader, it became necessary to extend the programme
of study; the student then was not only to think
submittingly, but to think also for himself. It was
thus found necessary to teach him philosophy, and
inform youths having no experience of life with problems, often insoluble, and over which conscience and
reason ponder painfully in the glimmer of fearful
realities, the brunt of which, at eighteen, young men,
thank God, have not yet had to bear.

The programme of the *baccalaureate* thus became
foolishly encyclopedic. Overcrowding crushed the
memory of the candidate, and too often succeeded
only in turning out superficial scholars, whose real
ignorance was only equalled by their vanity and pre-
sumption. Being conversant with every branch of
learning at seventeen is the sure means of being
ignorant of everything at forty. It is not in colleges,
nor in gymnasiums, above all to youth, that superior

education, that is, true science, should be taught, but in universities.[1]

History, relying upon the experience of two centuries, will no doubt some day tell the result achieved by such a _régime_ in countries like ours, where it flourished without rival; it will perhaps then point out, a little too late, I fear, the danger of rather too compressive pedagogics, and too precocious initiation of the mind to sciences which it cannot grasp.

Discipline is a chain: it must moderate initiative, not destroy it. Philosophy is a generous wine: do not pour it into new casks, whose staves do not yet closely fit.

Is it not hard indeed to see our country, France, —that classical land of collegians and of elegant speech, making eighteen - year - old philosophers— France become the country that obeys least, and where philosophy counts most sceptics?

I was once, in France, talking with the professor of rhetoric of a private college, about that defect of secondary education; I frankly declared how indignant I felt with the development of critical spirit in young men of sixteen, and spoke with the less reserve, as my words met with a sympathetic echo from my interlocutor.

[1] See Appendix.

" That tendency to premature criticism is such,"
said he to me, " that it invades even our literary
studies. In examinations, candidates are always expected to give critical analyses. And being bound to
see them succeed, do you know what I am driven
to do? To train them up to it. I spend the first
two months of the year of preparation in teaching
my pupils a *formulary of criticism*, and devote the
remaining eight months to teaching them how to
use it."

What an aberration in pedagogics! The child
must believe; nature gave it that instinct; the young
man, that is, the adolescent, must admire: his age is
that of fancy and enthusiasm; let us leave to men
the severe and difficult work of criticism. Judging
is the right of mature reason, able to control itself,
alike to resist enthusiasm, and to emancipate itself
from prejudices.

IX.

RELIGIOUS INSTRUCTION IN THE PROGRAMMES OF SECONDARY
EDUCATION—ITS NECESSITY UNDERSTOOD BY GERMANS—
DISREGARDED IN FRANCE — PATRIOTIC FEARS ABOUT A
GENERATION EDUCATED WITHOUT FAITH — RESOURCES OF
FRENCH GENIUS, INDISCIPLINE SUPERFICIAL, DOCILITY
FUNDAMENTAL.

WHILE religious instruction is almost absent from
educational programmes in France, it is being carefully preserved in Germany as the indispensable
element of the gymnasiums and of all secondary
education. Read the diploma of maturity delivered
in any gymnasium to the pupil who has satisfactorily passed his final examination : the first words
are, "We hereby testify that the pupil of Roman
Catholic—or evangelic—faith is efficient in religious
knowledge." They do not ask a being of eighteen
to give a critic's opinion about the great religious
problems, and to have an opinion of his own ; but
they demand that he should know the traditional
teachings of the faith of his ancestors.

This is, however, what can be read in the circular

E

of the Ministers of Public Instruction in Prussia, relative to the branches of knowledge to be taught in high schools: " Religious instruction shall comprise,—1st, The history of the Bible, but chiefly of the New Testament; 2d, The Catechism, with the Scriptural passages and traditions which explain it; 3d, The Ecclesiastical Year-book, and complete knowledge of the principal hymns; 4th, Knowledge of the main facts contained in the Scriptures, chiefly in the New Testament (reading of various passages selected from the *original text*); 5th, Fundamental points of dogma and morality; 6th, Knowledge of the most important dates of the history of the Church, of eminent personages, and of the lives of the principal saints." [1]

Not a word of philosophy. No apologetics. No premature discussion; positive, elementary, well-defined teachings, such as become intellects yet fresh, and which must be strengthened by doctrine and not prematurely destroyed by criticism.

In Germany, as in all other countries of the civilised world, reason has brought about great public controversies respecting the various creeds; and perhaps no people have carried on such debates

---

[1] Lehrpläne für die höheren Schulen, nebst der darauf bezüglichen circularverfügung des Königlich. Preussischen Ministers der geistlichen. Unterrichts und Medicinal Angelegenheiten. Vom 17 März 1882.

with more profoundness and tenacity than the Germans. But the men of mature years, who have the
direction of national education in Germany, did not
even conceive that the door of gymnasiums should
be left open for the introduction of those terrible
controversies, suited only to intellects already capable
of personal reflection. Youth there is brought up in
some faith. No doubt the native docility of the
German race renders this easy. What could we not
obtain from a race impulsive, witty, critical, and
even cynical like ours, if we only knew how to
curb it by religious discipline, and if, instead of
fostering in it precocious incredulity, we taught it at
the outset respect for a creed! What ignorance of
human nature! How very foolish and imprudent!
In our land of common-sense, is it not lamentable to
see the lay masses, the society of the ruling classes,
doing their utmost to foment everywhere, with the
mob as with the youth of the higher classes, incredulity and scepticism, and—still more dreadful—
organising public instruction on such a footing that
religious faith, if ever it could perish, might be
doomed to decadence and death? What can be
obtained from a race without faith? and what other
faith could ever replace the Gospel in societies raised
by it to such an ideal of justice as no other religion
—not excepting the Jewish—could ever satisfy?

When man, in the maturity of his mind, rejects the dogmas, he preserves the morality of his destroyed faith; in spite of himself he still retains in his implacable criticism his conscience, such as education and religious instruction made it—he fells the tree and keeps the fruit. But what remains if the tree itself has been destroyed in the germ? We shall see, when under our eyes the race of beings devoid of conscience and ideal are grown up and have multiplied.

Science may teach us what is terrestrially useful; it will not give us the habit of sacrifice, nor will it make us unyielding in the performance of duty. We may make laws; we shall not have the strength to obey them; and those laws themselves will always be deficient from lack of justice, for they will rather be the expression of sectarian ideas than the formula of general interest.

Everywhere complaint is made of the indiscipline so noticeable, of all peoples, among the French. To hear certain detractors one would suppose that incapacity for obedience is with us a constitutional vice. I do not share in this opinion. I know my blood —the blood of my countrymen—it is generous, capable of the noblest impulses and of the most manly virtues; but care must be taken not to vitiate it. Nowhere, not even in that Germany whose passive

obedience is so much belauded, did I meet with more
docile natures, easier to control, than in France—
nowhere a more obliging, sometimes even more complete abdication of personal independence, in politics
and religion alike. But that docility proceeds more
from sentiment and from the heart than from the
head and reason ; then sentiment is fragile and fickle,
reason alone is firm and consistent. Let us not mislead or enervate our French reason ; it is the necessary brake and moderator of a nature too easily
excited and too freely communicative. May we not,
however, inquire if it is not being perverted—
poisoned with the venom of criticism, of scepticism,
of irreligion ?

Shall I be pardoned for addressing these reproaches
to those who lead the opinion of the country through
such nefarious paths ? My remarks are prompted not
only by wounded faith, but by the ardour of a far-
seeing patriotism. The violation, the mere disregard
of the essential laws of human nature in a nation,
will eventually and fatally lead that nation to ruin.
When sectarian passion succeeds in dividing the
people, in inspiring the laws, in ruling even the
institutions, it is not only civil war of minds, it fore-
bodes the close, the inevitable decomposition of society.

X.

THE degree of intellectual culture attained by a
country is the measure of that country's worth,
and there is no better criterion of such degree of
culture than the state of its higher education. Per-
using books and programmes, asking competent men,
professors or rectors, young or old students, for information, is not enough to form a correct idea of
the vitality of such education; one must see with
one's own eyes the working of those institutions
where it is in operation.

In Germany those institutions are called universities.

To know Germany, one must have seen those

powerful *foci* of universal science which train the *élite*
of thinkers and of learned youth, and whence spring
the ideas that stir opinion. It is with such ideas
that I travelled through the country.

I visited the venerable Saxon university at
Leipzig, founded in 1409, and where neo-Luther-
anism built the bulwark of its orthodoxy. Close
to Leipzig the Prussian university at Halle still
shows with pride the schools founded by Francke
and Lange. There it was that the most fanatical
pietism and rationalism fought their hardest battles.
Despite the popularity of Wolff, rationalism did not
prevail. Halle followed in the university of Wittenberg, where Luther and Melanchthon delivered their
teachings, and Wittenberg is now a famous school
of divinity, where more than 400 students annually
attend the lectures.

I saw the young and mighty university of Berlin.
Founded at the beginning of this century, it now
surpasses, by the number and fame of its professors,
and by the reputation it acquired in a few years, all
the other universities in Germany. Few are the
students who do not deem it a great honour to spend
a few quarters in that celebrated school, and to
inscribe in their book (*Anmeldungs Büche*) the name
of some of its teachers. I also saw the Hanoverian
university of Göttingen, justly renowned by its

faculty of law, and to-day so proud to reckon the
great Chancellor of the Empire as one of its quarrelsome students. I went to the gorgeous Bavarian
university at Munich. The vanity of a king took
pride in giving its buildings a more than princely
majesty, and sheltering that queen, whose name is
Science, under a roof bearing the appearance of a
royal abode. I also visited the university of Tübingen, in Würtemberg. There the two Catholic and
Protestant faculties of divinity live peaceably side by
side like two sisters; 150 Catholic students of divinity and 300 Protestant students there display a
fraternity unaltered by difference of doctrine. Noble
example, to which the sectarian minds of many other
countries might well be directed !

Germany is to-day the classical land of universities.[1] There are, no doubt, elsewhere elementary
schools, colleges, lyceums, professional and special
schools, lectures on high political studies, even faculties that Germany might envy, but nowhere can we
meet with universities equal to hers. In the Empire[2]
to-day there are twenty-two : thirteen in Prussia and
the duchies or annexed provinces — Berlin, Bonn,
Braunsberg, Breslau, Fribourg, Greiswald, Halle,
Heidelberg, Kiel, Königsberg, Marburg, Münster,

[1] Deutsches Universitäts-Kalender : Berlin, 1882.
[2] See Appendix B.

and Rostock; one in Saxony—Leipzig; one in the
duchy of Saxe-Coburg-Gotha — Jena; one in the
grand duchy of Hesse—Giessen; three in Bavaria—
Munich, Würzburg, Erlangen; one in Würtemberg—
Tübingen; one in Hanover—Göttingen; one in Alsace
—Strasbourg.

These twenty-two universities are so many active
centres wherein science is perpetually mooted. They
mean a staff of more than 2000 teachers, and an
army exceeding 25,000 scholars. The identity of
organisation, and the fraternity existing between all
the universities of the Empire, allow of the students
passing from one university to another, to repair to
Berlin, to Leipzig, to Munich, to Halle, or Tübingen,
there to listen to the greatest professors, and thus,
as the *companions of duty*, to make the tour of the
Fatherland, as those in our own country pass from
workshop to workshop, when making what is termed
their *tour through France.*

Such is in Germany the vitality of university
institutions, such is the cultivation of knowledge,
that the university is sufficient of itself, and by the
power of the interests over which it rules, can itself
create a town.

Just as there are industrial and artistic towns,
military towns, and purely religious, maritime, com-
mercial, and manufacturing towns, so there are beyond

the Rhine—and that is a characteristic feature—
towns purely academical,—Göttingen, Jena, Tübingen,
for instance.

It is in such cities that we must sojourn if we
wish to examine closely and alone the peaceful
whirling of intellectual life in the educated youth
of Germany. In Berlin, in Vienna, as in Paris,
scientific activity, though very considerable, is lost
in the buzzing and bustle of life ; the noisy laughter
of those who enjoy life, or the painful groans of those
who exhaust their strength in earning bread, are
better heard than the deep buzzing of labouring
thoughts ; there the attention is more easily disturbed by the game of worldly intrigues or political
ambitions than by the persevering and intelligent
labour of man struggling with the unknown, winning
victories over ignorance and error, and silently training disciples who will walk after him in the ways of
light and truth. The mind perceives well that only
which stands alone, detached, in relief, on a quiet
horizon.

I never better comprehended true scientific activity than in those small German cities, peopled with
professors and students, and where the university
is everything.

They are generally ancient cities, of medieval
appearance, with their stronghold, their houses with

two or three storeys protruding one above the other,
and their steep pinioned roofs, pierced with a score
of bull's-eyes. The ditches of the old ramparts are
filled in and transformed into green gardens. Gigantic
trees cover them, and the patrol pathway is now a
shady promenade, where meditative minds may meditate as they please. The old fortress is dismantled;
it has lost its ruthless appearance; it is no longer
the shelter of the warfaring lord and of his armed
followers; it has become, as at Tübingen, a library—
the arsenal of science. Do not conclude, however,
that military force has disappeared; it has only
changed its aspect and tenement. Look at the plain
below, a short way from the little city; you see that
large edifice, which combines the appearance of a
palace with that of a fortress: it is the barrack.

The university city is quiet and gay. The Germans resisted the French mania of enrolling, of
secluding all. The student is left free; without,
as with us, entering the worldly whirling, he has
preserved his gaiety and the genius of his twenty
years. He is free from the sneering scepticism of
those prematurely old, who never had either an ideal
or a belief. He is a dreamer and a realist, little
caring about austerity, and preferring to obey nature
rather than to control it. German students are
quarrelsome, and far from abstemious—in fact, in-

capable of bearing a grudge to their beer even for a day: that beverage is severe enough to those who abuse it; but the Germans are free from a spirit of revolt.

Certain university towns are notorious for the turbulence of their students—Heidelberg and Göttingen, for instance. There duels are of frequent occurrence; more than a hundred are yearly recorded. They are a deep-rooted custom, remains of the war-like barbarity of the people. " Take care when in Göttingen," smilingly said to me a Berlin student, " not to elbow in the street, even accidentally, a *Bursch-enschafter.*" Quarrels between students are settled at the half-yearly vacation, before the holidays. The last weeks are indeed weeks of blood. On Wednesdays and Fridays, carriages are seen at dawn starting for some neighbouring village, carrying the champions ; they return with drawn blinds, bringing back the wounded.

The ordinary *Mensur* very seldom endangers the life of the duellists, who are provided with a steel scarf and a metallic network, protecting both the neck and the eyes. The rapier is not pointed at the adversary, but wildly brandished, so as to strike the skull and gash the cheeks. The nose, being the most prominent part, is in great jeopardy. If it come unscathed out of the contest, it considers itself lucky.

However large the cut—such is the peculiarity of opinion—it is an ornament in which the student takes pride. He does not conceal it; he proudly shows it as a sign of bravery, and as authentic proof of his having received the baptism of the sword.

In the university town, restaurants may be found everywhere. The inhabitants seem to be entirely devoted to the professors and students, and to consider themselves born solely to lodge, feed, and quench the thirst of their guests. Nothing can be more interesting to an observer than the inspection of the halls where youth and its teachers regularly come to spend several hours daily. There are met with all sorts of persons. Two well-defined types, however, are noticed among the students—those *whose sole object is mirth and enjoyment*, and the *hard-working and laborious youths*. The former, quarrelsome, with martial features, cheeks full of scars, wear small, peakless, coloured caps, stuck over the eyes, and go about flourishing their sticks, always followed by their lion-dogs; the others, impecunious, saving, and diligent, inelegantly dressed, wear their hair long, do not trim their beards, and live upon fifteenpence a-day, get up early, attend five or six lectures, and deserve by their assiduity to become the favourite disciples of some celebrated professor. The one type dwells on its adventures, its duels, its feasts; the other only

talks of science, of examinations, of its dreams of
the future.

Two types are also noticeable among professors:
the one, taciturn, reads his paper and gravely empties
his glass in silence; the other resumes, at the restaurant, before a small circle of disciples, his lecture on
philology, Arabic, old French, or history. Some live
retired in a lonely house; you see them pass every
morning, at the same hour, through the same streets,
on their way to their university, and every evening
taking a quiet walk under the big hospitable trees,
that seem to have grown there purposely to shade
them.

Thus, a century ago, lived Kant, in a little street
at Königsberg.

" I don't believe," says Henri Heine, " that the big
clock of the cathedral went through its visible task
with less passion and more punctuality than its
compatriot, Emmanuel Kant. To get up, drink his
coffee, write, deliver his lecture, take a stroll,—everything had its appointed hour, and the neighbours knew
it was exactly half-past two o'clock when Emmanuel
Kant, clad in his grey coat, his Spanish reed in
hand, followed the road leading to the little avenue
of lime-trees, which, to this day, in remembrance of
him, is still called the philosopher's avenue." [1]

[1] De l'Allemagne.

A life devoted to science requires an almost mon-
astic regularity. No one more resembles a Benedic-
tine friar or a monk than a true *savant*. Science is
like God from whom it proceeds; it absorbs and
isolates those who love it.

Some fine morning the little town becomes animated. All the houses are decorated with flags; from
every window emerges bunting of various colours. The
stranger, surprised, wonders who is the official party
about to visit the place. Gala carriages, in which
are seated students serious and silent as state ministers, cross at full gallop the streets ordinarily so
quiet. It is the *fête* of some university association.
On such occasions, everybody drinks, eats, sings, and
enjoys himself, from the tenth hour to sunrise next
morning. The old students being invited, rush from
all parts of Germany; and during the two days the
feast continues, you may see old fellows with grey
beards wearing the red, green, or blue caps as at
twenty, and fraternising with the young *Fuchs*.

Nothing can sever the ties of fellowship existing
between German students. Those whom wealth or
talent has placed in high positions do not forget
their less fortunate companions. Not a few, I daresay, to-day congratulate themselves upon having worn
the same brick-red cap that adorned the head of the
Chancellor, when he already displayed at Göttingen

his good luck and quarrelsome disposition by fighting scores of successful duels !

The students who have become *somebodies* are not forgotten in the university town. The houses where they lived are pointed out, their memory preserved from generation to generation. The landlord takes care that a marble slab, where the traveller may delight in reading the name of a great man and the date at which he was studying, shall be fixed to the wall. Not one of the celebrated men of Germany of the last century—Goethe, Heine, Müller, Humboldt, Fichte, Hegel, Bismarck—but has his commemorative stone.

Those working cities, in the widest acceptation of the word, seem to assist the work of thought. There are found the calmness of solitude and a bracing intellectual atmosphere ; there laborious students love to live ; there, slowly, patiently, far from the agitation of public opinion, so oppressive in many places, are achieved those works of criticism, of philosophy, of philology or science, which do not always solve questions, but often present them in a peculiar light—works truly independent, bearing only the stamp of the free genius of their author and of his indomitable patience.

The art of vulgarisation, so developed with us, is hardly cultivated beyond the Rhine, for it requires a communicative nature and a lucid mind—qualities seldom met with in Germans. In France, we write for the masses; scholars in Germany write only for that small public likely to feel an interest in their works and to judge them with a competent mind. Their works, important by reason of the subjects treated, are not elegant in style; they are, as a rule, the result of long study. So testify the productions of such philosophers as Wolff, Kant, Jacobi, Fichte, Schelling, Hegel, Herbart; of divines and critics such as Paulus, De Wette, Schleiermacher, Sertorius, Neander, Bruno, Bauer, Ewald, Moehler; and of historians like Müller, De Ranke, De Preller, and Mommsen. The writings, the books, are but the means of scattering abroad the master's word—of diffusing and spreading his teachings, and of winning over fresh disciples from other rival universities.

When a master-mind reveals itself by the power of its word, and chiefly by originality and newness of conception, it quickly rallies around it the young and impulsive. If the new doctrine shocks received ideas of religion, of philosophy, or of criticism, the war breaks out, fruitful mental war, in which the passions sometimes delay the progress of truth, but wherein also truth in the end succeeds in destroying the reign of obstinate routine, of false traditions as well as the tyranny of personal systems, systems always narrow, even those followed by genius.

The battle-field is sometimes one university only, sometimes several rival universities, and even the whole of Germany. Rival professors carry on the contest from afar, and the numerous learned reviews are opened alike for defence as for attack. The German—unless he belong to the ideal race of his great poets or great thinkers—is ignorant of niceties of form, of delicate irony, and of hidden meanings. When his heavy temperament enters the arena, violent words accompany his arguments, and are rapidly hurled, in the midst of polemics, like so many heavy stones. The champions have the appearance of wrestlers in a country fair. Their genius does not always preserve them from such displays of violence, and three centuries of culture and civilisation have not altered the actuality of the ' Table Conversations ' of a Luther, which to this day have remained classical in the fatherland of the man whom Germans delight in styling their *great reformer*.

XI.

UNIVERSITY BUILDINGS—THE STUDENT IN THE UNIVERSITY—
THE MASTER'S LECTURE—THE STUDENT LATE IN ATTEND-
ANCE—UNIVERSITY DISCIPLINE—ADMINISTRATIVE ORGAN-
ISATION OF THE GERMAN UNIVERSITY — CONSIDERATION
ENJOYED BY THE UNIVERSITIES: THE BRAIN OF THE
COUNTRY—THE SOUL OF GERMANY CHIEFLY REVEALED BY
THEM—GERMAN STUDENTS AT THE INAUGURATION OF THE
MONUMENT OF ALBRECHT VON GRÄFE IN 1882.

THE buildings devoted to science in Germany—from
the *Volksschule*, where the child of the people learns
to read, to the university itself—attract attention.

The university is sometimes an old convent, as at
Leipzig; a princely palace, having the appearance of
a fortress or vast mausoleum, as at Berlin; a modern
monument of high style, as at Göttingen, at Tübingen,
at Munich. Under these different appearances the
university always preserves a lordly air. It has the
calmness of a convent, and never loses that religious
silence which so well befits those assembled to think
or to pray.

Thousands of students rush through the long

corridors at the lecture-hours, no more disturbing the quietude of the place than do laborious swarms of bees that of their hives. Round the edifice are enclosed flower-beds—lilac and laurel-thyme bowers, large chestnuts and lime-trees—reminding one of the gardens of Academus. The lecture over, the student does not find himself in the streets ; he may at leisure walk through the beautiful promenade destined for his use, there to discuss with his comrades the lecture just delivered and its problems. At Berlin and at Leipzig, during the *academic quarter of an hour* (*akademische Viertel*) between two lectures, he may, at about nine or ten o'clock, take a breath of fresh air before resuming his morning task.

The porter's lodge is a kind of silent restaurant ; there the student quietly plays a game of dice, writes his letters, chiefly towards the close of the quarter, when his purse begins to feel light, and eats a slice of bread and ham, to which he adds a matutinal glass of beer. The most diligent, anxious to secure seats near the professor's chair, bravely bring their own breakfasts, which they eat there, no surprise being excited by it, so natural does it appear to Germans to eat and drink when feeling hungry or thirsty. This, among a thousand others, is a feature that displays in the German race a complete lack of the sense of propriety, of what we in France term the *convenances*.

The German acquires in individual freedom what he loses in civility. He takes no notice of his neighbour, and feels no offence at a breach of propriety in which he would be the first to indulge.

This rule holds good except in the case of students who happen to arrive late. The lecture once begun, the door is not considered open. He who then enters does not break any written regulation, but he seems to defy opinion, and runs the risk of being received with murmurs. Most students, by timidity or by respect, refrain from incurring such reprobation. The words of the professor and the attention of the pupils seem as inviolable as a sacrifice in a temple. Gradually the lecture-room gets filled. The students come in, their portfolios under their arms. They always sit at the same numbered table, crossing over tables and seats to reach it, and open their writing-books, prepared to write at the dictation of the professor. The professor enters last, without any ceremony. He hangs his hat and coat on the same hooks as his disciples. The usher with the bright chain of office is unknown here. The chair is a simple platform. No glass of sugary or even pure water; only a piece of white chalk, to illustrate the lecture on the black-board, which is always placed close to or behind the teacher. No phrases. He resumes his subject where he left it off the day before, only anxious to teach, desirous to satisfy the avidity of those who listen to him, expecting not to be amused but to be taught.

The German student requires facts, not words. No similarity between him and the Athenian with curious ears. He, so musical, who delights in the harmony of his great composers, does not seem to suspect that speech is a melody. Science for him is a mute algebra; it is composed of equations, and all he asks from the professor is to set free the unknown quantity. He at times applauds by violently stamping both feet on the ground, like the beating of drums. For my part, I prefer our clapping of hands, more noisy, perhaps, but more noble.

Those hundreds of young men, stooping over their note-books, listen rather than judge,—they believe their master rather than discuss his teachings. Their mind is docile; they practise the words of Aristotle—

"Oportet addiscentem credere."

To seize and appreciate all this one must be Voltaire's countryman. I never could discern in their eyes or on their lips the least sceptical or sneering smile. It is true that the organisation of universities in Germany enables the student to attend the lectures of any professor he may choose. He is the free pupil of a free master of free science. No obstacle debars him from the apprenticeship of high culture : neither regulations, nor customs, nor even money. He can cheaply enough spend his university years in any of the cities of the Empire, from Breslau to Munich or Vienna, from Heidelberg to Leipzig, and take his seat beside any chair at his pleasure.

The partisans of university tutelage can hardly understand that school of German freedom, nevertheless it trains some of the most docile students I have ever seen.

The more I like and admire independence of mind and character in a man who, by dint of work and maturity, of enlightenment and virtue, has become worthy of it, the more foppish and disastrous in its consequences do I consider that precocious Voltairianism that causes young minds of twenty to criticise and rebel against all that is taught them.   These newly enfranchised ones, ardent to judge all and to shake off all yoke, are not long in sowing their wild oats ; it is then not unusual to see them, in their weakness, embrace the pseudo-wisdom of those sapless believers who, devoid of vigour, are afraid to think for themselves, and of those citizens who, wanting in courage, describe as order their surrender into the hands of absolute power.

All the greatest scholars have begun by being disciples : they believed in a master whom their genius sometimes surpassed. All the greatest figures of history placed their energy and their faith at the service of some noble and holy cause : they learned to obey !

The student is sometimes ticklish on the score of patriotism. On one occasion at Berlin, a professor of philosophy was lecturing on the history of education in Prussia. He dwelt, with that impartiality which is the first duty of a historian, on the parsimony of a Prussian king, whom he was blaming for having during his reign too much stinted the budget of public instruction. Some expressions of discontent, rather discreet, were heard. The professor, speaking more slowly, went on in an impassible tone, his eyes fixed on the malcontents. The lecture over, the bulk of the students—they were more than two hundred—greeted him with an ovation,—their protest against intolerance and chauvinism, in favour of liberty and science.

The teacher in the university does not limit his task to public lectures ; he takes care at more intimate meetings to assemble around him the most diligent students. The object of these groups of the *élite* is not only the teaching of science, but of scientific method itself. The question is no longer that of becoming acquainted with acquired results, but being trained to scientific investigation and the practice of tuition. At these meetings, the ordinary name of which is seminaries (*seminar*), the master lets the pupils speak; he teaches them, if the study be history, how to decipher ancient documents,—if the subject be old French or old German, how to interpret the texts. It is the application to the various branches of knowledge of that which is common with us in regard to physiology, anatomy, or chemistry; it is the professor throwing open his laboratory or his hospital to some preferred disciples, and initiating them more closely into his methods of research and the processes of his personal genius.

The student receives from the university not only his intellectual formation, but the character of his public behaviour. He is more than a citizen of the German fatherland, he is the son of *Alma Mater*. With his title of student he receives his code of school-discipline. If he misbehave; if, in any way, he dishonour the dignity of his rank; if he insult his comrades or his masters; if, perchance, in an inebriated state, he has occasioned a public scandal,— if, in fine, during the half-year of study he has been absent for any length of time, and without the rector's permission, from the university town, he must answer for all before the rector, the syndic, and the university senate.

The punishments vary from a simple warning to formal exclusion. Between these two extremes there is a fine not exceeding a pound, imprisonment, and threat of temporary exclusion.

On the walls of the vestibule and the large hall of the university are hung four large black-boards (*Schwarzes Brett*). The first is for matters of interest to the students, and announcements emanating from the students themselves ; the second bears the names of the various professors, and indicates in which hall they lecture ; the third the subject of each professor's lecture ; the fourth is used for official communications issued by the university authorities. On the last-named are posted the juridical verdicts applying to the conduct of offending students. Every morning when the stream of students pours afresh into the university, they gather round the black-board ; read the news ; the dates of elections for the various associations ; the invitations from one university to another ; the hour, the day ; the name of the hall wherein is to take place that which the students call their *Commers* or meeting. The black-board is the official gazette, the record, the organ of the university.

These details are sufficient to show that the German university forms in the State a corporation endowed with a real autonomy. It is not a vast machine wherein the professors, entirely at the mercy of an autocratic minister, and compelled to follow programmes which alike prevent the flight of thought, and slowly dig the track of routine, are reduced to the condition of mere springs. It is a moral being. It enjoys the right of property; is empowered to recruit its members as it pleases—to administer its own interests, under the control of the State; and can, as shown above, exercise over the student a disciplinary action of rather vast extent.

The administrative organisation of the university is republican in form, elective and aristocratic—the highest authority being the academic Senate, at the head of which is the rector, who represents it, and is its executive power. The rector and the members of the Senate are alike elected by the universal suffrage of the teachers. The administration of the finances and of justice, however, is intrusted, under the jurisdiction of the Senate and the rector, to three special functionaries, elected for life—the judge, the secretary, and the quæstor. To these secondary agents belongs the care of collecting the fees of matriculation, and of the various registrations and examinations, and the sharing of them amongst the various teachers.[1]

[1] Cf. De la réforme de l'enseignement Supérieur. K. Hildebrand. Paris, 1868.

The true autonomy of those republics, as Herder used to call them, would be misconceived, were the positive ties of subjection and of subordination which unite them to the State unacknowledged.

Fundamentally the university is a State institution. The imperial shadow hovers above it. Every university has its curator, its chancellor, its commissary, selected usually from among the notabilities of the province. The curator seldom interferes with the internal administration of the university : his duty is to plead the cause of the university before the State, and to secure in its favour the liberality of the Central Government. Princes—kings themselves—do not disdain the patronage of a university. The Grand Duke Charles Alexander is rector of the university of Jena ; the Crown Prince of Germany and Prussia, a most munificent rector of that at Königsberg ; and the King of Saxony, a most generous rector of the university at Leipzig.

The public esteem in which universities are held in Germany extends to the doctors whom they create. Nothing can be compared with the respect which surrounds the *doctor*, and more especially the *Herr Professor*. That feeling not only exists in ideal pursuits ; it finds expression even in public life. Public opinion sees in them the enlightenment of the country : it sends numbers of them to the higher chamber

among the representatives of the empire. If we consult the directory of the deputies to the Reichstag,
we shall find, amongst four hundred members, more
than eighty doctors. The doctors thus represent in
Parliament the aristocracy of intelligence, as others
represent that of the soil, of birth, of fortune, or of
commerce.

Here we discover an instance of the evolutionist
tendency of the Germans. When social forces are
set in operation in the country their tendency is not
all-absorbing. The mania, the fury of centralisation—
that disease of all young nations like the Slavs, as
also of old ones like oriental races—is not yet prevalent in Germany. There custom has not sacrificed
power to ideas. The State would never presume to
violate the traditional autonomy of the learned corporations—to assert towards them a right of supervi-
sion, of dismissal, of suspension, or of appointment to
the various professorial chairs. The internal life of
our French Academy gives a pretty correct idea of
that of German universities. It seems as if German
people considered universities to be the brain of the
country. At home, we daresay, the brain of France
is a city, Paris, caring little as to where are the heart
and the arms of our country. Paris is more than
the brain! it is the universal motor. In German
universities is the brain of Germany. The heart is

everywhere, wherever patriotism breathes. As for the arm, it is of iron : it is authority armed and administrative, waging no struggle against the various social forces to absorb or exclude them. No force must be destroyed : all are sacred. The supreme law of life is that they should harmonise together and concur — indissolubly united in the universal progress of nations and of mankind. In Germany that law has received its practical application. Germany did not become feverishly excited by the powerful expansion of the forces which take the lead of modern civilisation and humanity—science, liberty, and commerce. No other cause but her national ambition can cause *her* serious anxiety.

Of this ambition German universities are not the least ardent *foci*. Thus to know the soul of Germany, the life of that active people which the university attracts—which she recruits from among all classes of society, amongst which she establishes relations of absolute fraternity—must be carefully watched. The superior culture of science, without destroying the natural distinctions of birth and fortune, creates above them a higher unity, wherein the first places are occupied by the most diligent and the most intelligent. And when, on the day of some university festival, those youths, with their martial appearance, march in solid ranks under the banners of their twenty corporations, escorting their masters, the people rush to the windows as on parade-days,— as on the days of grand military reviews,—not less proud to contemplate the youth of their *élite* than their Emperor, their princes, or their soldiers.

This I observed at Leipzig at the anniversary of the King of Saxony, and at Berlin in 1882, on the occasion of the unveiling of the statue of one of the university and medical celebrities of Germany.[1]

That last spectacle is still present to my memory— more than four thousand advancing in columns, with unfurled banners. The leaders of each association, with drawn sword in hand, opened the march, mounted on white steeds. The bands filled the air with their warlike harmony. After assisting at the inauguration of the statue, the *cortége* in silence took the way to Königsplatz, where stands the column commemorative of the victories of Prussia in 1864, in 1866, in 1870. The bands had then ceased playing. A national song,[2] grave and deep, suddenly broke the silence, pouring forth from a thousand throats. Upon

[1] Doctor Albrecht von Gräfe.

[2] Hab und Leben   Our fortunes and our lives
Dir zu geben   To give thee
Sind wir allesammt bereit.   We are ready.
Sterben gern zu jeder Stunde,   Death is always nigh,
Achten nicht des Todes Wunde,   We disdain death,
Wenn des Vaterland gebeut.   If our country call us.
     —*Allgemeines Deutsches Commers Buch.* Lahr, 1882

a sign given with the sword, the national song was succeeded by the song of the students, with the gay burthen—

" Gaudeamus, juvenes dum sumus."

.   .   .   .

The crowd then immediately dispersed in silence.

That scene wrung my heart with unspeakable anguish. In my patriotic sadness, I was thinking of the youth of my country. I asked myself why it was that our youths at home did not, like Germans, range themselves in line of battle, under the flag of true science, round the monuments of our glories, or at the foot of some mourning statue of our lost provinces ; and I considered how, in a near future, our younger people could be formed into a family united closely in the worship of truth, of freedom, and of the fatherland.

XII.

ASSOCIATIONS OF STUDENTS IN THE UNIVERSITY—BASED UPON
RELIGION, SCIENCE, PATRIOTISM, AND WARLIKE SPIRIT—
TYPES OF SUCH CORPORATIONS—THE *ALLGEMEINE DEUTSCHE
BURSCHENSCHAFT* — ITS PRINCIPLES — ITS STATUTES — THE
SCENE OF INCORPORATION — PATRIOTIC ADVANTAGES OF
THESE ASSOCIATIONS — THE LEADING MEN OF GERMANY
BROUGHT UP IN THEM.

THE grouping of students in divers associations is one
of the most interesting characteristics of university
life. It is only in those associations that such life
is seen in full activity; and it is by going deeply
into the secret of their organisation that we shall
acquire a correct idea of the spirit that animates
German youth.[1]

Of these associations I counted large numbers in
every university—twenty-five at Göttingen, twenty
at Halle, more than thirty at Berlin, and more than
forty at Leipzig. To the *ensemble* of the university
they are what the various arms are to the army of

[1] Geschichte der Pädagogik. Karl von Raumer, 4 Band. Güter-
sloh, 1874.

a country. Their variety does not impair their unity, it nourishes it; indeed, religion, science, and fatherland, such is the sacred tripod on which they all rest.

The idea and the sentiment of the fatherland are predominant in the *Burschenschaften*, and in the *Corps* which are recruited among wealthy and titled students. Particularism met with its stanchest adepts in the *Landsmannschaften*, to-day wholly on the decline. Their star has been dimmed as the sun of the Empire has risen.

The cultivation of science gave birth to literary, mathematical, philological, medical, and other associations, composed chiefly of diligent students, future scholars and professors. The religious idea itself brought about the development of theological and Christian associations, such as the *Wingolf*, the *Missions*, the *Suevia*, and the *Ascania*, which rally together the Catholic students of Germany.

Instead of declining with time as institutions out of date, these associations multiplied themselves. Those of which science is the main object have attained a wonderful stage of development; and though the last born, they occupy to-day the first rank among universities.

I had the curiosity to peruse the statutes of the one that has played the most prominent part, from the beginning of this century—I mean the *Allgemeine deutsche Burschenschaft*, which might very correctly be termed the German universal brotherhood. Its constitution, which dates from the year 1818, affords an idea of all the others—patriotic, religious, and martial spirit being therein most forcibly set forth.

The following are its principal clauses and by-laws :—

§ 1. The German universal brotherhood is the free association of German youths scientifically trained in the higher schools of the country ; its basis is the relation of German youth to the *future unity* of the German nation.

§ 2. The German universal brotherhood, being a free corporation, adopts as the pivot of its collective action the following universally acknowledged bases :

    a. Unity, liberty, equality of all the brothers amongst themselves ; equality of rights and duties.

    b. Application of all mental or physical forces, German and Christian (*christliche, deutsche*), for the service of the fatherland.

§ 3. The communion of all the brothers (*Bursche*) in the spirit of its principles presents the highest idea of the German universal brotherhood—viz., the union, in the same spirit and the same life, of all the German members.

§ 4. The association will thrive only when it has best realised the image of the fatherland, *free and united*, when its members, brought together in one free alliance, in accordance with equality and the requirements of national life, have obtained such a knowledge of life as to fully realise the majesty of its original beauty.

The corporation is ruled by a president, whose assessors in the management of business are: an orator or speaker (*Sprecher*), whose chief duty is to speak in the name of the association, to convene its meetings and preserve order in the sittings; a secretary (*Schreiber*); a president of the school of arms, charged with the maintenance of order in fencing practice, and the care of the flags and weapons belonging to the association; a hall-president, who selects the places of meeting for the *Commers* and the banquets; a treasurer, who watches over the financial interests of the association; and the *Pfleger*, whose functions are the welcoming of strangers, the showing of hospitality to them, and the seeing to the wants of the sick.

The incorporation has an air of ancient solemnity.

The candidate must be of German nationality, a Christian, thoroughly honourable, guiltless of any offence against the civil law or the by-laws of the brotherhood. He must not belong, or have belonged,

to any association whose principles and objects are
opposed to the principles and objects of the *Burschenschaft*. He addresses a written application to the
secretary. That official communicates the same to
all the members at a general meeting, and, in order
that all may be informed of the fact, causes it to be
posted in the meeting-hall. It is the right and the
duty of every brother to inform the president of any
objection to the acceptance of the candidate. If, in
the course of a fortnight, no opposition is offered,
the incorporation is proceeded with.

The scene merits description.

The brothers are seated at a table in shape like
a horse-shoe. The book of the constitution, *Commers
Buch*, is placed, closed, in front of each member. A
motion of the sword commands silence. The speaker
of the corporation rises and addresses a few words of
welcome to the new member, who stands up before
the meeting.

The secretary rises in turn, and, in a slow
clear voice, reads the usual words of reception :—
" You are now in the presence of the honourable
assembly to pronounce the vow that will introduce
you into our midst. I, the secretary, ask you, in
the name of the association, solemnly and publicly,
Do you recognise the thought and spirit which ani-
mate our constitutional charter ? Do you recognise

the thought and spirit which guide our fundamental
laws and give them power and credit ?   Do you
belong to the German nation, and do you acknowledge that, without a patriotic life, without personal
participation in the good and evil fortune of the
fatherland, our association could not achieve its aim ?
Do you declare yourself ready to defend with your
body and soul, within and without, the principles
and existence of the brotherhood, so that, if required,
you would not hesitate to stand or fall with the
brotherhood and the German people ? . . . If so,
place your pledge in the hand of the *Sprecher*."

The new member, extending his hand to the
representative of the corporation, replies " Yes."
Henceforth he belongs to the society of *Burschen-*
schaften.

The equality is absolute between titulars.   They
are brothers.   They " thou " and " thee " one another.
They assist one another as seconds in their duels.
The only differences between them are those of
experience and the length of time during which
they have been members.   At the end of a year
and a half, their acceptation is definitive ; at the
end of the second year, they may be elected members
of the *bureau ;* and, after three years' membership,
president.   Such differences do not lead to the subjection of young members by the old ; the worth of

the individual is reckoned, not the duration of his membership.

Every member is bound to take fencing lessons twice each week at the school of arms.

The duel is the mode of settling all questions of honour between students and those bodies which have not abandoned fighting. It is thus the duty of every member to be able to defend himself, to protect his comrades, and to fight for them or for the association.

The corporation holds *fêtes*, the object of which is to assemble, at least once a-year, all scattered members, and to rekindle the patriotic, religious, and fraternal feelings of the brotherhood.

These customs, like the spirit that gave them birth, are still as vivid in the midst of German universities as on the morrow of Jena. Certain of them have grown old, but the spirit remains young. The new *Burschenschaft* lately created has preserved the characteristics of the old one; its sole object is the removal of abuses, duelling, the oppression of the young members by the old, and certain excesses of student life.

I have just been reading a recent pamphlet [1] and some numbers of the 'Universal Gazette' of the German brotherhood. Therein are set forth the

[1] Die neue Burschenschaft, von Eug. Wolff: Berlin, 1883.

same principles, patriotic and moral, scientific and
warlike, which presided over the foundation of the
first *Burschenschaft*.   Observe them in their sober
eloquence!

1. Promotion of the national spirit, without party
politics.

2. Study of student history.

3. Scientific spirit.

4. Principles of moral conduct.

5. To live according to one's means, and never
break one's word of honour.

6. Development of bodily exercises: gymnastics,
fencing, swimming, &c.

7. To work as much as possible for the suppression of duels.

As we see, patriotism is still warm as ever, and
the taste for the sword quite as vivacious; religion
remains in honour, and science occupies a larger
place only to inspire fresh ardours and a new religious exercise.

Not a few, perhaps, will think this simple and
archaic; but with what are we to replace the fatherland, religion, science, martial spirit?   When religion
disappears, negations, indifference, and scepticism
take its place; science may still progress, but her
terrestrial flash will not prove sufficient to light up
the void left by the disappearance of God.   To ener-

vated patriotism succeed destructive political passions, and to martial spirit effeminate customs.

The men who laboured for German unity, who enlisted all their soul, all their force, all their genius in the service of that cause, were members of the *universal brotherhood*.

I have deemed it useful to give such information to my fellow-countrymen, and to describe the cradle in which our enemies, the great men of Germany, grew, and in which to-day are growing those whose ambition it is to become the heirs of such men.

XIII.

To thoroughly understand the high civilising power
of the universities in Germany, it is indispensable to
form a correct idea of higher education in the modern
world, as also of the institutions wherein it is being
taught and imparted.

Higher education comprises the universality of
science; it embraces all human knowledge, whatever
its object; the phenomena and the laws of nature
which experimental reason observes and declares.
It embraces man, intelligent, active, and free, and

God Himself, whom metaphysical reason and conscience reveal and explain. Divinity and philosophy, metaphysics and positive sciences, systems
and facts, doctrine and history, literature and languages, individuals and societies, all belong to its
truly encyclopedical province. Nor is this all;
certain arts of a more ideal order, or more necessary
to human life, the practice of which often requires
minds of the first class : painting, sculpture, architecture, music, agriculture, warfare, are also comprised
in the boundless kingdom of higher education, such
as it is understood in our civilised societies. That
kingdom, in fact, contains all branches of knowledge
likely to form leading minds.

It is the bright atmosphere whence emerge the
élite of thinking humankind; the labourer who tills
the soil and makes it fruitful, embeds the streams
and the seas, digs tunnels and pierces isthmuses,
makes inland seas or grows palm-trees in the desert,
shortens distances and brings nations into closer
contact; the learned, who know how to calculate,
to measure, to weigh the various forces, to fathom
the earth or unveil the mystery of the skies, to
discover the great law of universal evolution, to
surprise the secrets of life and the means of curing
its miseries; the historian, who brings the past again
to life, and shows us its forgotten features; the

philosopher, who gradually discovers the laws of the
mind and of truth, of æsthetics and of the beautiful,
interprets human beliefs and the arcana of God Himself; the jurists, who seek for immutable justice in
human intercourse; the great artists themselves, who,
by harmony and light, transmit to the ear or to the
eye of man the emotions whose ideal excites and
intoxicates him.

In the middle ages intellectual culture was much
more limited, men having then but a feeble idea of
the immensity of the universe and of the power given
them to conquer it; nevertheless, viewing the programmes and the organisation of universities in those
days, no doubt can arise that the middle ages had
foreseen the universality of higher education.

All knowledge was then comprised in the four
faculties, the synthesis of which formed the great
universe of science—the faculties of arts, divinity,
law, and medicine. The first, with its famous *trivium*
and *quadrivium*,[1] is a remote sketch of the various
sciences that gradually germinated in the fruitful and
always extending field of human intellect. Grammar
became philological studies in Greek, Latin, Sanskrit,
Zend, Persian, Arabic, Hebrew, Chaldean, Ethiopian,
Egyptian, French, German, English, &c. Arithmetic

---

[1] The *trivium* comprised grammar, rhetoric, and dialectic. The
quadrivium, arithmetic, music, geometry, and astronomy.

gave birth to algebra, differential and integral cal-
culus; geometry has been completed by trigonometry;
and astronomy, elevated to the superb function of
celestial mechanics, is no longer satisfied with observ-
ing the transit of the stars through the meridian, but
fixes and ascertains their trajectory through immensity. Music has been increased by the adjunct of all
the great arts that belong to æsthetics, and affords to
cultivated minds the noblest of emotions. Medicine,
since the great discoveries in biology, has unveiled
quite an unexplored world which our forefathers did
not even dream of; theology itself, which we might
fancy immutable, has reached wonderful proportions.
Essentially dogmatical in the middle ages, it first
became exegetical, when new-born philology put in
quite a fresh light the text of Holy Scriptures, then
historical, when historical research in its investigations into the life of the various nations and of mankind at large, brought to light the universal and
perpetual phenomenon of religion.

Nothing shows better the progress of the culture
of the mind than this simple comparative glance at
higher education amongst ancient and modern nations.
They both consider it as universal; but what a difference in the universality of each! With the ancients,
education may be likened to a lake, the banks of
which being limited, are easily explored; with us it

is like a shoreless ocean—the farther you explore it,
the vaster it appears. Genius is no longer a beacon
on the shore ; it is a star, shining above the reefs, in
the immensity of the skies : it no longer shows the
port—the port no longer exists. It only shows the
way through the rolling and stormy waves. Knowledge is infinite ; man who pursues it dies in the midst
of the immensity. What he explored is nothing, being easily measured. What remains to be discovered
is unlimited : in fathoming it, imagination and reason
draw back confounded. Nevertheless mankind goes
on without rest. Some irresistible attraction carries
it towards truth. It lives only in order to learn, and
learns only to rule over this world, the prey given by
God to its devouring and sublime curiosity.

There are now among enlightened nations, two
kinds of public institutions for the diffusion, the culture, and the progress of higher education—the high
schools and the universities.[1]

High schools present everywhere a double character—they are special, that is, exclusively limited to
certain branches of general knowledge ; utilitarian,
that is, having in view some more or less immediate
practical object. Their tendency is to obtain increasing influence in modern civilisation. From year to
year their number increases, as the province of know-

[1] See Appendix F.

ledge extends its limits, as men become more energetically intent upon learning, as the utility of science becomes more obvious through the increase of wealth, security, and comfort. Agriculture and commerce, forestry and mining, mathematics and history, literature and political economy, fine arts and warfare, inspire all nations with growing interest. Special schools are everywhere founded for training men capable of directing and managing the forces at work in the field open to their activity.

Universities differ from high schools precisely in these two respects,—instead of one branch of knowledge only, their aim is to reach all its branches, to constitute a synthesis thereof: instead of giving to studies a professional direction, they aspire to pure science, and instead of cultivating the latter in view of some practical application, they cultivate it for itself.

Knowledge and ability: these two words explain the aim of human life. The one might be engraved on the frontispiece of the *Alma Mater*, the other be written over the doors of all high schools. In universities are trained great speculative minds, in high schools great workers. In the former, discoveries are made; in the latter, they are usefully applied. The first is the realm of enlightenment, the second that of activity.

The ideal perfection of the organisation of higher education with civilised nations depends upon the prosperity of universities and high schools. Alone universities could not succeed in achieving practical training; but they excel in raising man to the level of general knowledge, without which the cleverest specialist will always, even in his own pursuits, be wanting in broadness of views and solidity.

The example of England testifies to the disadvantages of a want of equilibrium between the professional education given in high schools and the more theoretical teaching of universities.

In that country, the land of traditional and haughty aristocracy, there are two famous universities wherein education, divested of all professional character, is limited to high literature, to pure mathematics, to philosophy, history, and theology. Oxford and Cambridge are aristocratic schools, chiefly frequented by wealthy and titled students, who receive there a general culture—a kind of universal and disinterested science. The middle classes, through want of means, are obliged to avoid the university, and to enter at once the schools which give professional training for the various liberal careers of barrister, doctor in medicine, engineer, &c. The positive spirit of the Anglo-Saxon race thus remains deprived of counterpoise in classes wherein ideal is like unto an untilled

soil. In Great Britain there are, no doubt, clever men
in all professions; but, as a rule, there is a complete
absence of philosophical tendency, the result of which
is general mediocrity.

The fashion to-day is professional and high schools.
All nations, Germany excepted, seem to obey that
fashion.   Everywhere—in England, in America, in
Italy, in France, in Russia—high schools are founded
and multiplied.   Evidently modern nations feel the
necessity of subdividing labour in order the better
to carry it out.   They fully grasp the immense task
assigned to their activity; they know full well that
of themselves they can do but little, but that in
applying with intelligence the boundless forces of the
universe to the earth, wherein they display themselves, they will be enabled to transform that earth
and to rule it.

With that object it is that schools of agriculture
are founded, and that all States endeavour to train
up, under the denomination of engineer, the great
worker, the true Titan, armed no longer with muscles
and tools, but with the very forces of nature—electricity, steam, motive power.

As nature gives up its secrets, and genius penetrates the mechanical physico-chemical conditions of
life, specialists are required for such studies. So we
see appearing schools of botany, zoology, general

physiology, of organic chemistry, of histology. Medicine is compelled to subdivide itself into twenty different branches. The same remark applies to literature, history, philosophy, political economy. The study of one language alone, from its origin, is enough to absorb the life of any stubborn investigator. Knowledge not only widens but *deepens*. Each point requires for its treatment a phalanx of searchers.

Such is, in my opinion, the primary cause of the extension of special high schools.

If we observe this intellectual impulse of contemporary society, we shall soon come to the conclusion that it will eventually and fatally result in the breaking up of the vast unity of general knowledge; and that in fostering too energetically the practical applications of science, it will gradually dry up the inspirations of genius, to which theoretical science alone can give wings and flight.

Great discoveries are but the work of enterprising theorists, who lead the way for men of action. No specialists were they—mathematicians like Leibnitz and Descartes; geometricians like Pascal; a-priorists or fathers of audacious hypotheses, like Lavoisier, Lamarck, Geoffroy, Ampère, Claude Bernard. I am certainly not simple enough to suppose that we could ever have a nursery wherein to plant and grow great men at will; still, it is the duty of those who organise education to prepare the ground for those germs which are God's reserve. And the best ground for ensuring the development of the mind is universal education.

Do not let us prematurely restrain the horizon of the mind: however remarkably gifted a man may be, his tendency will always be to limit his task. The work that his genius is destined to produce is like the Pyramids, large at the basis, narrow at the summit: as it proceeds it becomes limited. Nothing can ever make up for the want of a vast primary culture; that is why universities must be kept up side by side with special schools.

In my travels through Germany, I tried to ascertain how far that country had succeeded in solving the problem of universal intellectual culture.

These dissertations are, in short, the result of impartial observations.

XIV.

IT must be freely granted that in no people in the
world, among the most intelligent and the most
learned, is universality of knowledge so carefully cultivated as in Germany, nor does it possess, for its
practical furtherance, better organised or more powerful institutions. Nowhere do universities better
justify their traditions, their grand old name of
Studium generale, of *Alma Mater.*

These works of a century, full of aspirations ; these
living cathedrals of Christian science, the style of
which is still more daring and grandiose than the
masterpieces of Gothic art—the domes of Cologne,

Westminster, and Notre Dame; this organisation of
the *omnis rei scibilis*, which once made Paris, verily,
the school of the world,—are still extant on the other
side of the Rhine.

The decline of the middle ages, in which they were
born, did not lead to their ruin; whilst the advent
of the modern world renewed and strengthened them.
Nothing could prevail against them: neither religious
struggles, nor the Reformation of the sixteenth century, nor the incredulity of the *philosopher kings*, nor
rationalism, nor free-thought, nor the gigantic strides
of modern science, nor political transformations. They
went on prospering in spite of all; and when we
examine the intellectual life of Germany, the twenty-
two universities of the Empire appear to the observer
like the culminating summits of its learned organisation.   These twenty-two summits form, in the
region of the mind—like a distant group of lofty
mountains dominating the plain below—real water-
sources wherefrom are filled the higher reservoirs of
modern thought, and which, by means of properly
embanked canals, distribute to the lower regions the
spring-water of universal science.

To-day, as in the middle ages, the whole of human
knowledge is, in German universities, divided into
four chief faculties—theology, jurisprudence, medicine, and philosophy.

At first sight one is puzzled to understand how these simple special titles can contain the whole world of higher knowledge. It is obvious that, obeying the instinct of preservation so conspicuous in their genius, the Germans wished to faithfully preserve the traditions of their forefathers. This classification calls to mind those works of Gothic art, less correct than expressive, which express grand ideas and divine sentiments by awkwardness of attitude and incorrectness of outline. In the middle ages theology represented the severe harmony of divine and human science; jurisprudence was but Roman law imported by the Church and purified by canon law; medicine, a great deal more than nowadays, imposed itself upon poor mankind, always trembling before suffering and death; the faculty of arts represented all the scientific knowledge of those days. Then, such a curriculum was thought to be sufficient; to-day, that curriculum would be thought far too restricted. To us it only seems like the cradle wherein mankind slept its first sleep and attempted its first steps. Being now fully grown, it requires space and a larger field of action.

This is what the Germans have fully understood: they have, in consequence, thoroughly modified and extended the ancient educational frame. Instead of using the saw and the axe, they have gathered fresh

materials; instead of sapping and destroying, they
have completed and repaired the old edifice; instead
of building a new one, they have merely enlarged
the old.

Should we see in this an intelligent devotion to
the past, or the irresponsible instinct of conserva-
tion? I know not. The Germans have respectfully preserved alike their institutions and their
monuments of the past. To slowly transform, to
destroy nothing, such seems to be their rule of
conduct. Go through Germany, almost everywhere
you will meet with the old town-hall with its belfry,
the old church and its tower. And if fancy leads
you to the top, you will still see there the old watch-
man in his cell open to the four winds: as in the
past, he still strikes the hours and sounds the alarm
in case of fire; this, the only difference, he no longer
uses the horn, as of old, but the telephone and the
electric wire.

These quiet processes of transformation would
hardly suit our enterprising and impatient genius;
in bringing them under notice, it has not been my
object to present them as models for imitation. I
am no critic, I am but a faithful and sincere artist;
I abstain from admonishing or blaming; I am satisfied with describing the picture as I saw it. All
things carry with them their own teachings.

German universities have preserved the numerical elements, the titles, the etiquette of their ancient organisation, though they have pretty thoroughly modified its ordinance and its spirit.

Thus the faculty of philosophy, which now corresponds with that of arts, is not, like the latter, a kind of preparatory faculty to the three great professional faculties of theology, jurisprudence, and medicine. It now obtains a footing of equality with them. It has even assumed an encyclopedic character. The great hierarchy of sciences, based upon mathematics, and developing themselves, like the world itself, according to the rules of increasing complexity, from the inorganic kingdom, subjected to number, weight, and measure, to the kingdom of the highest form of life, such as exists amongst the higher orders of animals and with man himself, from chemistry to anthropology and sociology,—all this immense synthesis belongs to philosophy properly speaking, and constitutes that fourth faculty which contributes the most in giving to German universities their character of universality.

In Italy, as in France, the truly material distinction of *sciences* and *letters* has been adopted: pure mathematics, physical and natural sciences, or rather experimental and positive sciences, have been grouped under the heading of *sciences;* and philo-

sophy, history, literature, and languages, under that
of *letters*.

It is in vain that we seek for a meaning, or for
some kind of profound idea, in this aimless classification. Its only result, it seems, has been to break
up the great logical unity of knowledge, and to
contribute to the spreading amongst people of the
prejudice that true science is only experimental, all
the rest belonging to ideology, or to vain, idle fancy.

There is, on the contrary, profound wisdom in
considering all superior knowledge as a tree, whose
infinitely multiplied branches proceed from a common
trunk—philosophy.

Does not, indeed, every science, carried to that
degree of profoundness requisite to its cultivation and
teaching in higher education, revert to philosophy?

What is philosophising, if not seeing from above
and from afar, seizing the first principle and the
remote conclusion ? As there is a universal, abstract,
metaphysical philosophy, so there is a philosophy of
each science, and for all science in general. Philosophy
mingles with everything, and science is only perfect
as enlightened by philosophy. Confined to its tech-
nical processes, any science may be the object of a high
school ; but, if entering the great university unity,
it must assume the higher character of philosophy.[1]

[1] See Appendix E.

What would be thought of a literature content with admiring that which of yore was termed the literary beauty of a work? It may appropriately enough be praised as an art, as a branch of æsthetics, but not as a science; it is a matter of taste, of artistic feeling. Taste, then, is cultivated and trained by education; it is no more susceptible of being taught than is genius.

We have, indeed, at times experienced all that is conventional, arbitrary, empty, in that process which, wanting both scientific and philosophical method, can easily be misled,—that is why we gave *belles-lettres* and their study a more positive impulse, truly scientific and instructive, that removes even the very appearance of propriety in the wrong classification of sciences and letters. Literature is now more than a question of taste; it has become learned criticism. Instead of simply admiring the production, the masterpiece of a century, we now endeavour to explain philosophically the conditions and the law of its genesis; and instead of applying to the ancients modern feelings or contemporary ideas, we have succeeded in bringing to light their true physiognomy, without any addition of features foreign to them, and in them we have at last recognised the human mind, the same now as it was then.

The three professional faculties of theology, jurisprudence, and medicine, have simply been preserved in German universities. They meet three of the greatest requirements of social life. Everywhere there must be priests, legislators, and physicians.

In new-born and illiterate societies the priest presides only over worship ; the legislator is but an arbitrary judge, cutting gordian knots with the sword ; and the physician is but an empiric, ignorant of disease and how to cure it. Among civilised nations the priest is also a scholar, knowing what he believes, why he believes, and being well able to persuade or refute the ignorant ; the legislator possesses the science of law and justice ; the physician is a true *savant*, initiated with the mechanism of life—he knows how the clock gets out of order, also how to repair it if the springs be not broken.

The modern world has enlarged itself ; it does not exist solely under the direction of priests, legislators, and physicians, it also obeys the impulse of all those great workers whose object is to improve the earth and to adapt it scientifically to all the wants of civilised mankind.

How was it that the Germans, who so practically and wisely preserved and improved, strengthened and extended, the old educational frame of medieval times, did not add a fourth faculty to the three professional faculties ?

By true intuition of genius Leibnitz had foreseen its necessity; he dreamed of a new faculty, amidst contemporaries little able to understand him. He called it the economical faculty (*faculté économique*). Its province was to embrace the whole programme of our polytechnic and central schools, mechanical arts and mathematics in their generalities, as well as all that concerns the food of man and the commodities of life.[1]

Leibnitz's dream has not yet been realised on this point: routine has prevailed in the organisation of public education amongst all nations.

Since Germany herself has not followed the inspiration of one of her greatest men, I trust France, in one of those hours of initiative, the secret of which she sometimes has, may add to her faculties of sciences and of letters an *economical faculty*, such as was demanded by the great German thinker.

[1] Nouveaux essais sur l'entendement humain.

125

XV.

ISOLATION OF THEOLOGY IN HIGHER EDUCATION IN AMERICA,
IN RUSSIA, IN ITALY, IN FRANCE—RESEARCHES INTO THE
CAUSES OF THIS PHENOMENON — DUE TO THE STRUGGLE
BETWEEN CHURCH AND STATE—GRIEVOUS CONSEQUENCES—
THE LOWERING OF THEOLOGY IN FRANCE NOT RECENT—
TALLEYRAND - PÉRIGORD AND DIDEROT — ADVANTAGE OF
EMBODYING THEOLOGY IN THE ORGANISATION OF THE
UNIVERSITY — NECESSARY DISCUSSION OF PHILOSOPHICAL
AND RELIGIOUS QUESTIONS—TRAINING OF THE CLERGY IN
THE DIOCESE OF ROTTENBURG IN WÜRTEMBERG.

IF Germany was wrong in not completing the old
university organisation, other modern nations committed a much more serious fault—they reduced it.

In Russia as in America, in France as in Italy,
almost everywhere, the faculties of theology have been
eliminated from the encyclopedic organisation of knowledge. I am wrong : theology has not been suppressed;
it has been made, like the military art, a professional
faculty : it has not been destroyed ; it has been shut
up and isolated in schools—closed to the life of the
general public.

This phenomenon, which it would be difficult to bring to light, has had numerous, often quite opposite causes. On the one hand, the Church, at the sight of modern life, rising like a flood, did as Noah—she contrived to build her own ark, therein to shelter the race of her elect, her fighting phalanx, her divine book, all the treasures of tradition. On the other hand, growing unbelief refuses more and more to acknowledge the highly scientific character of the Christian doctrine and of Catholicism; by a sort of secret instinct it has guessed that the safer means of throwing discredit on religion and depriving it in our new civilisation of the consideration that attaches to all that is intellectual, is to reduce the priest, the teacher of eternal truth, to the position of a minister of worship.

In reality it was the struggle between Church and State that contributed most to separate theology from human sciences. In the Church, the spirit of preservation commingled with a feeling of unheeded or wounded dignity; in the State, incredulity and absolutism have always brought about the same results.

Wherever the *régime* of the union of both powers exists—wherever the Church and the State, as subject or as mistress, remains united, in Austria, in Germany, in England—religious science continues to be an integral part of higher knowledge, and theology occupies the first place in universal organisation. With nations where the struggle has been more hardly fought, it tends to disappear. In Italy, theology has been excluded from the twenty-one new universities of the young kingdom, and has been obliged to seek refuge in large seminaries or in half-ruined cloisters. In France, official and public opinion have but little regard for supernatural science, but men of talent there often reawaken the honour of faith by their eloquence and their culture. We still possess five faculties of theology ; but those faculties, frequented only by amateurs, have no influence on the training of the clergy ; they are but the ghost of a great name, the last threatened *débris* of an old *régime* that is fast falling to pieces.

In the United States—that country where practical reason is everything, and where, as a matter of course, religion is looked upon as one of the highest social forces—religious science could not succeed in becoming an integral part of university teaching, because of the innumerable variety of denominations which rule over the conscience. The university of Yale at New Haven, and that of Harvard at Cambridge, are the only ones possessing a faculty of theology. The former is Unitarian, the latter Congregationalist. Religious science is everywhere taught in large ecclesiastical colleges, usually founded by members of the same denomination and adherents of the same belief. The States number more than eighty-three theological seminaries for the intellectual training of doctors and preachers.

Placing ourselves outside of all narrow views, considering only the prosperity of the State, of religion, and general culture, we shall regret the fatal concourse of events which in most modern States gradually deprives modern religious science of its traditional place. The State thereby loses, for it is altogether profitable to possess an intelligent clergy in close communion with national life ; but religion also loses, for, after virtue, nothing in the eyes of the modern world honours it more than true science ; general culture also loses, for it counts one branch the less in the tree of universal science.

The new professorial chairs, under the name of *History of Religions*, can no more fill the void than the history of medicine can supply the study of medicine itself.

The decadence of theology in the organisation of universities is not of recent date. To retrace its progress, we must go back a century ; and in order to discover what a narrow idea of religious science existed in governmental regions in France at the time of the Revolution, we must peruse attentively the *Speeches and Reports on Public Instruction (Dis-*

cours et Rapports sur l'instruction publique), pro-
nounced and read in the National Assembly during
1791 and 1792, and in the Convention.[1] As an
instance, let us take the passage in the report of
Talleyrand-Périgord[2] relating to schools for the ministers of religion.

Isolation of theology, reduction of divine science
to vulgar professional science, the lowering of the
functions of the priest, which become purely political,
like those of any public official—nothing is wanting
in the statement of the sceptical bishop. "Theology,"
according to him, "ought not to be regarded as a
science. Sciences are susceptible of progress, experiments, discoveries; theology, that can only be the
knowledge of religion, is foreign to all this; like
religion, immutable, it is averse to any innovation.
The object must be, not to extend its province, but
to keep it within its own limits, beyond which subtle
ambitions too often endeavoured to go in times of
ignorance."

Diderot went even further. "A country wherein
theology is not reduced to two pages," says he, in
the midst of his blind philosophical prejudices, "is
threatened with the greatest disasters."[3]

---

[1] 'L'Instruction publique en France pendant la Révolution,' by
C. Hippeau.

[2] Ibid., p. 73.   [3] Pensées inédites.

These strange ideas have been spreading. They have flourished, to the detriment of peace and truth; and, thanks to the patronage of a sectarian policy and a sectarian science, have succeeded in persuading the largest numbers that religion is an obstacle to the free and intellectual evolution of man.

However imperious their reign be now, I cannot submit to their tyranny. What I observed in Germany enables me to foresee what a well-balanced society should be composed of.

Freedom remains the only true solution of the greatest difficulties with which we are beset.

It is she who rules over everything in the universities beyond the Rhine.

The State does not pretend to teach there its own theology, its own philosophy, its own science, its own politics. It authorises the teachings required by public opinion or by the wants of the population, with the welfare of which it is intrusted. Are the Catholics in a majority? they possess, as at Breslau, their own faculty of theology. Are the Protestants in a majority? they, in turn, have their Protestant faculty. Are the numbers equal? then, as at Tübingen, Protestants and Catholics alike have their own faculty.

As regards scientific and philosophical liberty, it

is seen at work in the faculty of philosophy. All practical interests are thus taken into account. Doctrines may, at will, battle against one another.

Are we to deplore this? By no means, if men respect themselves. The discussion of philosophical or religious truths has become, with us, a social necessity; and universities are the fit arenas for such debates.

If that noble arena, wherein the elevation of mind ensures the elevation of the contest, be not thrown open, discussion will seek others: it will descend into the tumult of the press and of the street. Quickly envenomed by the blast of party passion and hatred, it will soon lose, with its serenity, its consideration and its grandeur. We see that in France: no elevated question can ever now be decided. Violence alone commands attention. Insult and sarcasm having the last word, reason can but hold its tongue.

The best, the sure means, to withdraw religious questions from the discussion of the streets, is to give them the shelter of universities.

Must we, therefore, do away with seminaries in our own country? I do not think so; but, no doubt, valuable advantage would accrue from their being completed by regular faculties of theology, wherein the future priests, sent there by their bishops, would come to study. Divine science would once more find itself in vivifying contact with all human sciences. Like them, it must live; and to do this, it must commingle with the progressive life of human things. Isolated, it remains unmoved in its rigid formulæ—it crystallises. Cast into the ground, the formula becomes a living germ; it shoots, grows, transforms itself, assimilates. In passing through the ideas of Greek philosophy, what did not these simple words, " Son of God," theologically commented upon, produce? and what wealth did not Christian philosophy heap up, solely by the contact with oriental metaphysics, and by the sole development of a cultivated reason which knew how to draw logical conclusions from revealed principles?

This necessity the Germans have duly recognised. Nothing interested me more, from this point of view, than the system adopted for the training of the clergy in the diocese of Rottenburg, in Würtemberg.

The child destined for an ecclesiastical career pursues his classical studies at the gymnasium, or at the episcopal school, known under the name of *Nieder Convict*, and corresponding with our French lower seminaries (*petits séminaires*). On leaving either, the youth is ripe for the university; he is inscribed on the books of the faculty of theology, and goes to Tübingen for high theological instruction. There he finds a

house, founded and endowed by the late King of Würtemberg, where young theologians without means
receive board and lodging gratuitously, and live together under the guardianship of a director and several
tutors (*Repetent*), who watch over their labours and
their conduct. It is neither our system of indoor
pupils (*internat*), with its severe seclusion, nor that
of outdoor pupils (*externat*), with its unrestrained
liberty; it is a medium system, where a young man
can, without danger, begin his apprenticeship of
freedom, live as a brother with his colleagues of the
other faculties, and form with them intellectual and
cordial relations which, later on, will facilitate the
discharge of his pastoral duties.

At the expiration of his eight half-years—that is,
four years of hard study—the theologian who wishes
to join the ranks of the clergy repairs to the high
episcopal school at Rottenburg. Here he only spends
one year under stricter discipline, and in seclusion.
It is his higher seminary (*grand séminaire*). When
deemed worthy, he receives all the orders; he is taught
the professional science of priests, the liturgy, and the
ministration of the sacraments. At twenty-five years
of age he is ready to enter upon his pastoral functions.
If he should be observed to possess aptitude for
higher intellectual culture, he is sent back to the
university as tutor, there to undergo the doctor's

examination that will open a university career to
him. The priest thus enjoys the consideration that
everywhere, in Germany, is attached to the title of
doctor, and even to all who have received the baptism
of academic science.

In this is to be seen one of the most active causes
of the superiority with respect to erudition and
science of the German clergy over the clergy of other
nations. Similar conditions would everywhere produce identical effects; and we could not hope too
much in the future, if the organisation of higher
university education were again to favour Spain,
Italy, and France with those great minds who were
at once the lights of their Church and the honour of
the literature of their own countries.

XVI.

FREEDOM OF GERMAN UNIVERSITIES—ABSENCE OF PROGRAMMES —DEMOCRATIC GRANDEUR OF THE TITLE OF DOCTOR—HOW UNIVERSITIES IN GERMANY MAINTAIN THE UNITY OF KNOW-LEDGE—IN FRANCE, UNITY OF KNOWLEDGE IS PURELY ADMINISTRATIVE—OBLIGATION OF EVERY STUDENT IN GER-MANY TO ATTEND THE LECTURES ON HISTORY AND PHILO-SOPHY, WHICH FORM THE LOGICAL AND PRACTICAL UNITY OF SCIENCES — IMPORTANCE AND DEFICIENCIES OF OUR NORMAL SCHOOL.

LET us dwell upon one of the most important features in the pedagogic system of German universities—freedom.

The student is as free in Germany as the soldier is disciplined. In the university organisation, the individuality is as free and as much respected as it is crushed in the military organisation. In the army, passive obedience, blind, automatic, unswerving; in the university, spirit of initiative under broad rules, to the advantage of the last arrived student as to that of the first of the masters. If the army may be compared to a colossal machine, all the motions of which are geometrically regulated, the university may be considered as an organised living being, moving of itself.

No programme. Science is free, method is free, the choice of a subject is free, the professor is free, the student himself is also free. Freedom animates, vivifies, affranchises all.

Twice a-year the senate of the university selects and appoints the subjects to be treated by the professor, as also the lecture-hours. The teacher informs the students of this decision by means of a simple bill, written and signed by himself, and affixed to the *black-board*. The students thus warned must choose the lectures they wish to attend : they call at the quæstor's office to give in their names, and to pay the master whom they prefer. After this, they need only call upon him once to get their books signed. Thenceforth they are entirely free to be faithless or assiduous.

The eight half-years of the university career are crowned by the thesis, the examination, and title of doctor. Those who feel tempted by such glory find in that attraction the stimulus of a labour the more praiseworthy and fruitful that it is free.

The value of the doctorship is purely scholastic, but the very fact of its being optional adds still more to that value. Although it facilitates the entry into most professional careers, it is not a necessary condition. Purely honorific in its nature, it is only indispensable in medicine or for a professorship. It is simply the grand seal with which the university impresses those who, being initiated into higher knowledge, are thenceforth to belong to the intellectual aristocracy of the country. True title of nobility, the least of the people's sons may carry it as proudly as the son of a baron, of an earl, or of a duke carries his own.

This is a trait of true and truly great democracy. None can help admiring it, however little exclusive castes may be deprecated, and though intellect but scarcely secure its right place—below virtue, no doubt, but far above birth, fortune, and other things which men most boast of.

The consideration granted by public opinion to all the acknowledged servants of truth and science is one of the best points of modern civilisation in Germany. They are no longer the luxury of a court, the Mæcenas of an Augustus, some sort of Chinese mandarinate: they belong to the country itself, and are the independent members of a popular and independent class.

Might not such freedom be a danger for French youth? It is to be feared. The vivacity, the feverish ardour of our blood, requires, perhaps, the

yoke of programmes; and study gains with us by
being stimulated at frequent examinations by self-
love and emulation.

If only, whilst the student is controlled, the master
were left free; if he were not condemned to move in
the narrow circle prescribed by the programme, to
lecture without leaving the stipulated routine! But
no; he is forbidden to choose the subject best in
keeping with his tastes, to search the field whereto
his inspiration calls him. Such freedom of action is
only countenanced with the professors of our faculties; and why? Because, having no pupils, they need
not follow any programme, or coach up for any examination. And as one servitude will bring another,
the result is that science itself is enslaved.

Where, indeed, can it be free if it be fettered on
the lips and in the mind itself of the master, whose
function should be to impart it in its freshness to
the youth of a country?

What difficulties do not liberal ideas meet with
in order to get acclimated in our midst! So long
as science be a prisoner, nothing can be affranchised.
The liberty of science does not essentially consist in
the destruction of the State monopoly,—it consists
practically in the freedom of action of the teacher.
In every country where universities are open to all,
where the professor may teach as he pleases, how

and when he pleases, without having forced upon him a plan, a programme, a method, or a hand-book, —science is free.

It matters little that the State considers such institutions as being under its rule, if, whilst claiming that monopoly, it does not interfere to enforce its own ideas, the doctrines of a minister or of a party ; and if the student is not compelled to submit to a tuition that shocks his tastes, his convictions, or his belief.

Such is the case in Germany.

Nowhere, in the university, did I see even the shadow of an oppression of the mind or of the conscience. Free from all programme, the mind of the young man may freely aspire. The teachings he is about to receive are free themselves ; they are not the last words for the pupil. Science knows no last word. The proudest genius only leaves landmarks in the great road of truth.

As knowledge extends, and the immensity of science is unveiled, the mind anxiously endeavours to discover its unity. It follows the unique and all-powerful *Cause*,—hidden key of the numberless phenomena that take place before it ; but that inaccessible *Cause* cannot be penetrated, and man must resign himself to know but the harmony of phenomena, to understand but the ever simple law according to which they unroll themselves ; yet such is the

length of their chain, that it is not given to any one
mortal to hold alone the beginning, the middle, and
the end thereof.   It is, however, possible for a group
of men to associate in view of attempting that gigantic labour.   Universities were the result of such
associations, of the great want of intellectual unity.
Just as the circumvolutions of the brain are coiled
up together and form the organ of thought, so the
various sciences unite to form the faculties closely
grouped together in the university, thus establishing
the great organ of collective and national science.

That largely comprehensive unity is the phenomenon which particularly struck me in all German
universities.   In no other country does it reach such
a state of perfection.

In France, the unity of knowledge is purely administrative : it does not imply the living, organic
correlation of all the branches of general science.
The university of France is simply the hierarchical
battalion of teachers, from the Minister himself, who
holds absolute command, to the school-teachers, who
are like corporals.   Can those subordinate agents,
scattered all over the country, contribute towards the
unity of science ?   Our organisation by *faculties*
hardly succeeds in bringing together the few professors who are intrusted with the various lectures of
the faculty.

As for the pupils, it is hardly worth while to mention them. Those amateurs who frequent the lectures chiefly of the faculty of letters, are generally a great deal more anxious for fine speech and eloquence than for science and erudition. There exists no companionship between those conventional or chance students, who are past the age of enthusiasm, and whom no rivalry can bring together at an examination or at a competition. They do not exchange ideas : they elbow one another, but never form an acquaintance.

The German university does, on the contrary, efficaciously co-operate to the unity of universal science. The vast material organisation which assembles under the same roof, at the same hours, all the students for the various lectures in the four faculties, within which is involved universal culture, provides the professors with opportunities of knowing each other, of exchanging their views, and of placing at each other's service the mutual help of the science in which each excels. These relations become still closer, seeing that each professor in the university is called upon to arrange with his colleagues for the election of the rector, and that he may belong to the academic Senate, to the intellectual judiciary authority of the corporation. He is truly the living member of a living association ; his colleagues are not for him unknown individuals, whom he may pass without seeing; they are necessary co-operators in the grand work of higher education.

The same is true of the students, as regards necessary intercourse. In Germany we do not see those almost insurmountable barriers which in France isolate the students of the various faculties. There physicians, jurists, philologists, theologians, mathematicians, fraternise without distinction : they sit at the same *Kneipe* on *Commers* day, and between them there is not only an exchange of pleasant sayings, but a close contact of ideas that enriches the knowledge of all. I many a time witnessed those free and jovial conversations between theologians, philologists, mathematicians, and jurists, and I always ascertained that, in such intercourse of minds submitted to different cultures, ideas are enlarged, fresh horizons are unveiled, and the brain is fecundated.

Indeed, the concentration of various studies in the same establishment enables a diligent and anxious student to learn to attend the most varied faculties— from the lectures on dogmatical theology, Christian morality or exegesis, to those on Roman law, history, ancient or modern philology, or mathematics.

How many young men thus find their true vocation !

The wish of the parents, some awkward influence,

the birthplace, caprice, often causes a young man to engage in studies or to embrace a profession for which nature did not intend him. If he be at a special school where only one science is treated, or one group of homogeneous sciences, he can only follow one path. His intellect is, perhaps, misled for ever, and his future seriously jeopardised.

Whereas in the university, all sciences being in close union, all the divers professions being there represented, the hesitating young man will the more easily discover his vocation, and, to obey it, he will only have to alter his plan of studies.

And in order that this grand idea of the unity of higher science may not remain a vain word, but be faithfully carried into effect, it is necessary that each student be bound to enter for attendance a course of philosophy and history.

Philosophy and history are, indeed, the indissoluble tie of all sciences. As soon as, in any speciality, law or philology, medicine or mathematics, we rise to the philosophy of those particular sciences, —as soon as, leaving aside the narrow limits of the purely actual point of view, we search the past to write the history of a science,—we enter the very region where all specialities meet. Philosophy brings us to the study of the human mind, where all sciences have their primary source, and history shows us the vast stage of mankind where sciences only appear as part of general culture.

Thus in philosophy sciences find their logical, psychological, ideal unity, as in history they display their practical and real unity of action.

In France we possess a higher school, where, despite obvious lacks, there appears in the unity of the same institution that beautiful universality of science, such as is seen in the twenty-two German universities.

The *École normale* is no doubt the richer soil of French intellectual culture, the nursery where are reared the most learned minds : it is that which provides the faculties with their professors, literature with writers, science with pioneers, history with the erudite, and philosophy with thinkers. It owes all this still less to the excellence of its professors, to the diligence and the intellect of its pupils, than to a certain feature of its own organisation.

Of all French schools, there is not one that has united so many divers sciences within the same precincts. Such a gathering brings forth some sort of luminous atmosphere wherein the mind breathes more freely, and that increases tenfold the original vitality of the collected sciences.

The French higher normal school, compared with German universities, presents, nevertheless, a double inferiority : in the first respect, it does not, like them, possess a faculty of theology ; secondly, it is a boarding-school, open only to a few privileged persons.

Therefore religious science is no longer represented in the *cénacle* of French scholars, and thus the pupils of a school with narrow doorway easily succeed in forming a narrow Church. It is not easy, even for the largest minds, to escape from the results of the ignorance of an essential part of knowledge, or to help considering themselves as a race of *élite*, solely because they possess a cerebral circumvolution more developed than the rest.

K

XVII.

IN a country of growing democracy like France, where public opinion tends more and more to become paramount, too much importance could not be attached to the organisation of science in all its branches, and to the broad education of minds in the full light of reason, without prejudice against belief or against reason itself.

The errors which prevail in the course of a century, and the passions which those errors have at times kindled in the public life of a nation, can often be ascribed to no other cause but the ignorance and false systems of the ruling classes. And as nothing favours more that *learned* ignorance and those false systems than the narrowness of superior instruction, we must, if we love our country, endeavour, to the best of our ability, not only to extend popular knowledge, but to organise truly superior knowledge, in its freedom, universality, and unity. Should we, to obtain that aim, need even to borrow from Germany, it matters little. The virtue of an energetic patriot cannot hesitate; for, when national interest is at stake, there is no room for vanity.

It is nearly a century since those difficult debates on public education were opened and produced either in the parliaments or in the opinion of our country —a century of attempts at organisation. Whenever France was shaken by some political or social commotion, the question of primary, secondary, or higher education broke forth anew, plans of reform multiplied themselves everywhere. On that ground parties engaged in the most relentless struggle, as though some secret intuition warned them that a triumph in that direction would bring about their ultimate victory.

That problem was, in turn, examined and studied by the National Assembly of 1789, the Convention, the First Empire, the Restoration, the monarchy of July, the second Republic, the second Empire, the third Republic; but none of the proposed solutions have yet fully satisfied opinion.

After a century of efforts, of attempts, and of progress, the question of public education is still pending. Even to-day there is not a man, anxious for the highest interests of his country, who has not a vague consciousness of the thousand desiderata suggested by the actual solution.

We should be wanting in justice towards our country if we did not acknowledge the flight of public education in France during the last century.

Popular education is being widely diffused. The school is everywhere; it is more and more the table served for all, and at which the son of the poor has his place, assigned and compulsory.

Two classes of beings formerly lived without intellectual culture—the masses and the women: the masses, on account of their poverty; the women, because of their weakness; both, on account of their servitude. The masses are still poor, but education costs nothing. Woman remains feeble, but truth raises her from bondage, and henceforward it will depend upon herself, upon the efforts of her mind, combined with her virtue, whether she becomes, in growing equality, the enlightened companion of man.

General culture has extended its limits beyond those assigned to it in dreams.

What a discrepancy between the programme which the Great Alcuin drafted out for Charlemagne, and that imposed to-day upon any bachelor of arts! How vast the distance travelled in eleven centuries! How broad has thought become! What surprising enlightenment in our world of ignorance and darkness! What a wonderful display of activity in all the branches of higher education! How numerous the new fires that have been kindled! How learned the division of labour, as the growing work of science required more numerous and more special workers!

We might doubtless speak with much reserve respecting the intricate causes which urged on the diffusion of education, prompted the indefinite extension of programmes, and brought about the necessity of instituting fresh chairs and special schools: this fact will nevertheless remain—minds are incontestably more enlightened. Our sky is brightening. Science is in superb evolution. Man is devoured with the passion of knowledge; his eye is surveying all horizons; his endeavours to penetrate the secret of all that is, of all that lives, is truly prodigious. He possesses true method, and, in his struggle with the unknown, not an effort is lost.

It will be seen that I am far from denying the merits of our public education in France. However, I should not act up to my convictions if I did not also mention its defects. It is a painful duty for me to expose them.

Primary education is deprived of religion.

Secondary education is foolishly encyclopedical.

Higher education is specialist in the extreme.

These are grave aberrations. They will produce, they have already produced, like all that is false, baneful fruits. The child without God never will become a man. The youth, crammed with an education without limits, will remain, in most cases, with but a superficial mind; and the specialist, on leaving the schools wherein he has been cloistered, will always be wanting in that broad and lofty spirit without which it is hard to conceive manly and superior reason.

As for the servitude that causes all our systems of education to be bent under the yoke of inexorable programmes, what regrets, what complaints does it not extort from all free-minded men! It is well to think of this. Programmes, in France, are a chain which lays hold of the child almost from the cradle, and grows with him, without leaving him for an instant, until when, become a man, he is considered fit to exercise some public profession. From the village school to the *licence*, programmes are there, strict, pressing, implacable. If they but bound the pupil—but they hold the master fast in their claws.

And so long as the master is not free, tuition is enslaved. No more disinterested science ; no more
initiative. Is it, then, surprising that, in this country
where natures have so much spring and vivacity, little
by little even the sense of spontaneity and originality
is eventually lost ? Self-thought and self-action are
leading qualities which, sooner or later, disappear if
not submitted to delicate culture.

We still live under the university organisation
devised by Napoleon the First. The whole genius
of this man is embodied in his woiks, with its wants
and its excesses, its militarism and its absolutism.

The corporation of teachers is but a branch of the
great administration of the country ; it is but some
sort of army, with its commanders-in-chief, its generals, its colonels, its captains, and its sergeants under
the high authority of the Secretary of State. Official
programmes are its war code. No initiative, either
for the professor or for the pupil. The one has but to
teach according to official programmes that which
the other has but to learn. There is no autonomy
in the staff of that army of workers. They are
recruited according to the orders of the central administration. Is there a vacant post ? The minister
alone is empowered to fill it : he is the great engineer.
If one of the wheels of the machine gets broken, a
fresh one is put in its place. This is what the body

of teachers is reduced to in a country where liberty is indeed found in the vocabulary, but can hardly be said to have as yet entered the habits of the people, and seems but the theme of speeches, or weapon in the hands of minorities or of parties anxious for tyranny and absolutism.

Strange! this country, so fond of liberty, only succeeded in producing an organisation subjected to the State, to power, without the least independence. Those legislators whose dream was to train modern man by imparting universal culture, only succeeded in creating more or less narrow specialities. This nation, the first among all to extol tolerance as a civic virtue, and to inscribe liberty of conscience in its code of principles, could not be brought to see in national education anything other than the means of ensuring the predominance of such or such doctrine, and, above all, of uprooting the religious faith of old.

It is impossible to point out more shocking contradictions. On seeing them constantly renewed, we ask ourselves in anguish, must we not despair of a country where practical sense meets with such affronts, and where errors, far from being corrected by experience, take deeper root, so as to become indestructible routine ?

However little we may be accustomed to search into the phenomena presented in the life of a people we never hesitate to look for them in national institutions.

Do you wish to know why the French mind is as we see it to-day? Study the mode of organisation of public education. Man always becomes what we make him. Is not the mind of French youth the result of our *régime* of national education? Its qualities, as its defects, have no other source. The doctrines which rule a whole generation can be traced to public schools. He who wishes to ascertain why such a generation thinks this or that, need only inquire what were the teachings of its masters.

For nearly half a century, French youth being imbued with spiritualist and rationalist philosophy, France remained spiritualist and deistical.

Religious science being banished from official programmes of public education, France became ignorant, indifferent to religious matters.

It is now more than thirty years since the larger half of our youth, in conformity with the system of *bifurcation*, was weaned from philosophical studies: the majority of cultivated Frenchmen fell insensibly into philosophical indifference; and positivism was, for a time, enabled to pretend to rule opinion, and to take the place of those high metaphysical doctrines which always were the honour of the French mind.

We devised the famous distinction of *sciences and*

letters, become with us the fundamental division of our public education, as though literature could exist without science, or science be conceived without literature: then sprang up in our midst a whole tribe of individuals whose pretension it was to know how to write. Write what? They do not trouble themselves about that. Like those ancient sophists who posed as masters in the art of devising arguments, they give themselves out as artists in that of putting words together. The former used to discuss for discussion's sake; the latter write for the sake of putting pen to paper. Their style is sonorous, resounding; their thought empty and vague. The garments are superb; the body they cover is a shapeless doll. Nowhere more than in France will you meet with those hollow professors of *style*, writing and speaking the more since they have nothing to say!

For the last few years, our youth has received an education whose circle, constantly widening, finally became universal, encyclopedical—the consequence of which was soon produced. The number of superficial minds, of sciolists, is on the increase; and never at any time were there to be found men who had studied so much and knew so little.

In the organisation of public education considerations of freedom were totally ignored. The result soon followed—the initiative of the mind was soon paralysed; and now nothing is so rare amongst us as an intellect capable of self-will and self-thought.

Lastly, the various branches of higher education were more and more subdivided, sometimes isolated, sometimes opposed, in special faculties, in high schools and establishments for indoor pupils: intellect soon followed suit, and became subdividing, isolated, and grouped into sects, political or religious parties.

To a judicious observer our country seems to be suffering from epilepsy—that mysterious and fearful disease whose outward manifestations are frightful convulsions, and whose secret cause is to be found in a deficient cerebral co-ordination.

It is truly distressing to acknowledge such infirmities.   It is not without intense pain that a true patriot free from delusion sees the evils from which his country suffers, knowing at the same time his inability to relieve them.   If austere truths were not preferable to all, I would espouse blind Chauvinism, that declines to acknowledge the evil, or the simplicity of those credulous minds which believe a speech or a book to be sufficient to cure everything.

If we glance over the history of public education in France, we see it divided into two separate periods:—

The first, that of the old *régime*, terminated at the

time of the Revolution with the old *régime* itself,
having lasted nearly twelve centuries. As regards
its corporations of teachers, its essential character
was the predominance of the Church and of the
clergy : the method itself, according to which education was then organised, betrays that predominence.
The *ensemble* and the synthesis of science was placed
under the absolute sovereignty of theology, which
ruled and inspired all inferior science. As for the
institution itself, its character was really that of a
corporation : it formed a sort of autonomous power,
recruiting its own members under the high patronage
of kings, bishops, and popes—sometimes even checking their authority.

The second period dated in reality only from the
constitution of 1808, whereby the despotic and military genius of the Emperor changed the university
corporation into a sort of militia, and made it an
administration of the State, under the name of the
Imperial University of France.

From 1789 to 1808 the ardent genius of the
Revolution did not remain inactive : the problem of
public education and its fresh organisation was being
constantly mooted, either in the Legislative Assembly
or in the National Convention. But theory, new
prejudices, the ignorance of practical wants and requirements, misguided the mind.

There were *littérateurs* and writers—not politicians nor men of action. They enacted laws, as one writes a book : they were the Jean Jacques, not the Lycurgus, of their time—simple enough to believe that a people could be made by dint of laws. They acted as though France did not exist before them, and as though the old *régime* could have been annihilated by a decree. More bent upon destroying than upon building, upon preventing an offensive reaction of the monarchical world than upon serving political truth and their country without prejudice—they ignored that which is eternal in human nature, and, proclaiming the rights of men, they never dreamed of reminding them of their duties ; they saw only the man of their fancy, not the man of reality, with his miseries and his vices, his criminality and his pride.

To be convinced of this it is only sufficient to read the three reports of Messieurs de Talleyrand, de Condorcet, and Daunou.[1] In these three documents which the new spirit inspired, and wherein are seen panting the tumultuous passions with which the world was and is still upset, it is easy to recognise the principles which even to this day rule in France all the organisation of modern education,—the omnipotence of the State, the servitude of education, the

[1] 'L'Instruction publique en France pendant la Révolution,' by C. Hippeau.

rupture of the great unity of knowledge, the increasing predominance of the scientific element in education over the literary and religious element.

What changes would occur if, instead of the omnipotence of the State, we could have the neutrality of the State—not indeed a neutrality synonymous with indifference, but one blending itself with justice, and ensuring the true reign of liberty and the exercise of common rights; if we only knew how to reconstitute the vast synthesis of universal science, and re-establish harmony between experimental sciences, philosophy and letters, theology and faith!

I willingly cherish that hope, though, at the same time, I dare not believe it will ever be realised. I know the fatal immobility of public institutions once established; and it is not necessary to have a long experience of life to know to what extent, everywhere, perhaps in France more so than anywhere else, routine tyrannically rules.

XVIII.

REIGNING IDEAS AMONG UNIVERSITY YOUTH—NO POLITICS—
LOVE OF THE FATHERLAND—PASSION FOR GERMAN UNITY—
THEOLOGIANS AND SOLDIERS—ANTI-SLAVS AND ANTI-SEMIT-
ISTS—THE MASTERS IN PHILOSOPHY—THE THREE GENIUSES
WHICH RULE OVER GERMAN THOUGHT—THE HISTORY OF
PHILOSOPHY—HISTORY APPLIED TO ALL SCIENCES—GEOG-
RAPHY AND PATRIOTISM—ANCIENT PHILOLOGY—RELIGIOUS
SCIENCES — THEIR ACTIVITY — RELIGIOUS BELIEF AMONG
GERMAN YOUTH.

IT is of the greatest importance to know the political
reigning ideas to-day in Germany, and especially in
universities the preferred doctrines in philosophy,
the sciences of predilection, the religious beliefs.
Assiduous intercourse with the university youth enabled me to satisfy my legitimate curiosity.

Here is the result of my observations.

Politics find no room amongst the students. With
them there is neither Socialist nor Conservative,
neither Unitarian nor Particularist, neither Liberal
nor Clerical. Do you not belong to some political
party? I often inquired. My question only provoked
surprise. They did not seem to understand me.

Germany is still far from having politicians twenty years old. Moreover, in that country I never remarked that morbid precociousness which is perhaps the most deplorable result of our French pedagogics.

On the other hand, I always found amongst German youth a lively love of their native land. I still recollect the enthusiasm with which a student spoke to me about his town of Meiningen in Saxony, and another of his mountains of Harz in Hanover,—with what simple joy they both cherished the hope of seeing them again at the next vacation.

This love of the native soil does not enthral their ideas nor restrain their impulse. Their country does not in their eyes and during life constitute the whole universe : it is a halting-place where they rest themselves from the fatigue of the journey, and gather fresh strength for advancing farther. I have never observed the dream of German youth to be the possession of a very little spot of ground where supreme felicity would be enjoyed in sowing their own cabbages and potatoes, and calmly passing away under the shadows of their oaks and firs.

German unity, such is the ardent passion that stirs all the university folks. It is patriotism in all its pride, its ambition, and its effervescence. The particularism of the various confederate states, though quite apparent in the nation, does not in any sensible degree modify the patriotism of trans-Rhinan youth inflamed by the very name of the German Fatherland (*Deutsches Vaterland*).

The idea of any kind of humanitarian cosmopolitanism finds no favour with them.

If you mention the United States of Europe to these positive natures, they do not smile—Teutons cannot smile—they burst out laughing. They consider the future without illusion. They foresee menacing struggles right and left. But knowing that in this world strength is the main factor of triumph, they cultivate strength.

That cultivation of brute force is displayed by all literate youth, in their quarrelsome customs, the frequency of duels, the practice of violent physical exercise, and, above all, their military predilection.

Every student wishes to be, and feels himself to be, a soldier.

I do not believe there is any nation amongst whose literate youth militarism is more universal, more perennial. Religious feeling cannot restrain this. Theological students are, like their comrades, enlisted into the army of the country. I remember having seen at Tübingen, during the vacations of 1882, more than twenty students of the Catholic faculty of theology taking part in the autumn manœuvres, thus devoting their time of rest to a patriotic duty, which in Germany suffers no exception.

The regiment, on its way through Tübingen, spent the Sunday in the little university town. The twenty students called on their masters, and, wearing the military uniform and helmet, observed with them that Sunday, as they were wont to do in the students' frock-coat and cap.

Is it because of their being so used to obedience? Is it the love of their country and their taste for arms? Is it reservedness of character? These are questions which I cannot answer; but I never heard any complaint against that rigorous law which brings every German under the colours.

Patriotic passion, amongst youths as amongst the people, generally fosters certain ardent sympathies or antipathies. In this respect, the students are the faithful image of the whole nation. The hatred of the Slav may already be detected. The Jewish question, Semitism and anti-Semitism, is heard with resounding echo amongst them.

Germans consider themselves at once as a nation and as a race. If they regard the Jew and Slav with repulsion, if they view the Latin with envious jealousy, it is that in them they see different and rival races.

The special hostility which Jews meet with even

from literate youths seems to proceed from patriotism and religious feeling. The Israelite is, by nature,
mixed with all, yet distinct from all. To me he
appears a being of a parasitical essence. He will
always be treated as an enemy by the organised
beings upon which he implants himself; and the
opposition he will meet with will be the more bitter
as those collective beings shall have a more distinct
perception of their own unity. This explains the
importance of the anti-Semitic movement in Russia,
in Hungary, in Germany, as also the indifference it
meets with in our own country.

Philosophical ideas did not seem to me to have a
very strong hold over the mind. The era of masters
is over. None now can be said to have opened a
new school; none, as in the days of Kant, of Wolff,
of Hegel, of Fichte, or of Schelling, exercise sway
over a whole generation. Throughout the whole
world, indeed, without excepting any nation, philosophy is passing through a period of decline. Where
is the powerful mind which opens new prospects
to contemporary thought by the creation of new
systems?

The believers look back to the middle ages, and
are compelled to go back five centuries to find a
master. With much trouble they endeavour to make
scholasticism appear younger, and to fecundate it with

the light of modern sciences. In Italy, some great minds, like Rosmini and Gioberti, have hardly succeeded in renewing ancient philosophy; in Spain, Balmes has made no school; in France, it is with much trouble that the high traditions of Cartesian spiritualism are still preserved; in England, positivism has deliberately shut the door against metaphysical researches having as their object Him whom it calls the *Unknowable*, and the province of philosophy is limited to the *Experimental*. In Germany, Lotze is the last of philosophers who enjoyed general renown in universities. Most professors now follow Herbart's doctrines.

All German philosophical thought is, in my opinion, dominated, and its bearings directed, by three great geniuses—Spinoza, Leibnitz, and Kant.

Pantheistic tendencies, which seek unity at all costs, and delight in erecting a system, belong to Spinoza. The prevalence of vast erudition and of a conciliating eclecticism is inspired by Leibnitz. As for psychological and critical problems, they originated with Kant, whose mighty works ponderously weigh upon the intellects which they divide into two contrary schools : the idealists, who, scorning experience, consider, like Hegel, their superb theories as the absolute measure of things ; the realists, who, subordinating the *subjective* to the *ob-*

jective, borrow from reality the rule of their speculations.

I fancy that to-day the university youth, which to-
morrow will form the ruling opinion of the country,
inclines to realism, to a certain unconscious panthe-
ism from which German minds scarcely ever liberate
themselves,—and, above all, to an eclecticism based
upon serious erudition.

In Germany, as in France, philosophy is influenced
by the development of experimental sciences.

Psychology is fond of borrowing from physiology;
and the antagonism brought about by Kant between
ideal and real, subjective science and objective science,
no longer troubles the mind; but scientific materialism has found more than one clamorous interpreter.[1]
Nevertheless these misguided intellects have succeeded less in leading German youth than in pro-
viding learned French materialists with weapons, at
a time when it was fashionable with us to believe in
the infallibility of German science.

The history of philosophy occupies the most prominent place : this alone suffices to show that professors are much more intent on exposing the various
systems than on teaching some personal one.   This I
observed at Leipzig, at Berlin, at Göttingen.

In high university chairs, materialist or positivist

---

[1] Büchner, Karl Vogt, Molescott, Fischer.

doctrines are left unrepresented. The rash speculations of thought are not nowadays viewed with high favour; philosophical tradition is, however, faithfully preserved.

Superior geniuses are not always given to a nation, to a century, or to a particular science. When they appear, all gather round their light and listen to their voice; and truth progresses. When they disappear, everything seems plunged into darkness. The honour of man is, then, to preserve the living tradition of their inspirations, at the same time preparing, by dint of work and exertion, the way for the genesis of a master.

I was struck with the extreme importance given to history in all particular sciences, and even in all questions—literature, law, philosophy, theology, philology, or exegesis.

Erudition is, for the German, a point of honour, almost a sort of scientific coquetry. In the solution of a problem, his aim is not only to satisfy his personal conviction; he further wishes to know since when and by whom the problem was propounded, and what various answers it obtained: he thus makes the history of the question that of the solutions; and it is only after this double preliminary work that he propounds his personal idea.

Such a method appeared to me to be singularly

wise, and apt to enlarge the mind, to prevent its becoming intoxicated by its own thought, and to enrich it with the thought of others.

Being trained to that intellectual process, students soon contract the habit of applying it to everything. I often had occasion to admire in them a breadth and moderation of judgment, which, I doubt not, proceeded from the large part assigned to history in the method of public education.

Sedentary habits are as injurious to the development of the mind as are stay-at-home customs to that of nations.   History causes the mind to make journeys, by compelling it to put aside its own thoughts, by bringing it into contact with other intellects, in other countries, with past civilisations in bygone centuries.

Therefore is history abundantly and profusely taught beyond the Rhine.

The following were the subjects of the various lectures at Berlin during the summer term of 1882 :—

Greek history, from the fourth century before Christ.
Modern history, from the sixteenth century to the Peace of Utrecht, in 1648.
Explanations of certain monuments, with bearings upon history and art.
Roman history and Latin epigraphy.
The history and topography of Greece and the Peloponnesus.

Greek mythology, with the interpretation of the art
works of the royal museum.

Latin and Greek palæography.

History of the Babylonians and of the Assyrians.

Interpretation of Assyrian inscriptions.

History of Germany from the interregnum to the
Reform.

On the form of international alliances.

History of Europe from 1789 to 1815.

History of German art from the sixteenth century to the
present time.

Geographical history of Germany.

History of Prussia from 1786 to 1815.

Modern history.

Such quotations need no commentary.

One of the sciences whose cultivation is foremost
is higher geography.

At Göttingen, in the year 1882—to mention only
one instance—more than 200 students flocked to
the lectures of Professor Wagner. He was then
lecturing on the formation of the soil on the German
shores of the North Sea. The method of the master
appeared to me well worthy of remark. He taught
as much by drawings and charts as by speech. All
he said he illustrated with various-coloured chalks.
In this way the constitution of the various strata
of the soil, the sources of streams, the woods, the
peopling of countries, were all made clear. Geolog-

ical laws were fully displayed on a small scale on one of the points of the planet, to the great admiration of the young listeners, who followed this scientific exposition as they would the various phases of a drama.

What a healthy food for patriotism are those lectures on profound science, by which youth learns in what providential ways the soil of the country was gradually formed!

Patriotism is also, not quite so obviously perhaps, the soul of another science held in high honour—philology.

No idea can be formed of the ardour with which the universities cultivate the study of old German. Erudition is not the only object, the sole fruit, of those archæological studies. Intercourse with the old authors preserves the freshness and youth of patriotism. The national genius existed already fully developed in those writers, who were the fathers of the language, and who, in immortal strains, recited the history and the legends of a nation, its victories and its disasters, sang of its dreams and its ambitions, expressed its feelings and its higher thoughts.

Religious science holds a distinguished place in most universities, not only because it occupies the leading place in programmes, but also, and above all, because, under the influence of esteemed and often famous teachers, it rallies a youth numerous and ardent.

There are more than 4000 theological students, scattered among the twenty-two universities of the empire, who in the mass of students form the most serious and diligent group. They it was who founded the *Christian Association*, whose members are distinguished by their white caps, with black, white, and golden stripes.

The activity of theological science cannot be denied. Every professor treats at least two different subjects. And as the smallest faculty of theology does not possess fewer than six professors, there are thus at least twelve lectures. At Leipzig, where the faculty of theology numbered fourteen professors, twenty-five subjects were being treated in the same half-year.

These are the titles of the various subjects studied during the summer vacation of 1882 : [1]—

History of the Church.
Epistle to the Hebrews.
Moral theology.
Epistle of Saint James.
Compared symbolics.
The Psalms.

[1] *Verzeichniss* der im Sommer Halbjahre 1882 auf der Universität Leipzig zu haltenden Vorlesungen.

The Messianic prophecies.

Epistle to the Romans.

Life and Doctrine of Schleiermacher.

Introduction to the Old Testament.

System of practical theology.

Biblical theology of the New Testament.

Messianic prophecies of the Old, and their fulfilment in
the New Testament.

The prophet Isaiah.

The idea of the covenant in the New Testament.

The minor prophets before the exile.

Hebrew poetry.

History of worship among the Hebrews, and its bearings
upon the criticism of the Pentateuch.

History of Christian architecture compared with the
requirements of the present time.

The Gospel of Saint John.

Add to this the practical labours accomplished in
the various associations of theological students—the
Theological Association, that of Preachers, that of
Missions, the Homiletic Seminary, the Catechetic and
Exegetic Associations, the Society of Ecclesiastical
and Archæological History—and some idea may be
formed of the prodigious intellectual movement of
which, in Germany, every faculty of theology is a
centre.

The encyclopedia of religious science is thus approached from all sides; and the students, who are
excited by an ardent wish for study, live under the
cross-fire of the thousand rays of the same science.

Of special religious sciences the most cultivated are, beyond doubt, exegesis and history.

Dogma in Protestant faculties appeared to me subjected to a thousand fluctuations, and to endless indecision. It varied from university to university, often even from chair to chair. The divers consistories endeavour in vain to preserve their reciprocal orthodoxy ; the professor keeps his freedom of action, so long as he does not irritate public opinion —a condition which he always finds easy to fulfil, if he but succeed in devising a formula preserving the basis of Christian faith.

One fact will give an idea of the extraordinary theological activity of German faculties. For the last century the life of Christ has produced more than sixty important works, amongst either Catholics or Protestants.

The following are the principal Lives of Christ published in Germany :—

J. G. HERDER.—The Saviour of Men according to our first three Gospels. Riga, 1796.

The Son of God, Saviour of the World, according to the Gospel of Saint John. 1797.

J. J. HESS.—History of the Life of Jesus. Zurich, 1822.

J. V. REINHARD.—Researches concerning the plan conceived by the Founder of the Christian religion for the welfare of mankind. Wittemberg, 1830.

A. BODENT.—The first and the holiest of human histories—Jesus of Nazareth. Historical and Critical

Treatise as regards Greek, Roman, and Jewish religion. Gemund, 1818.

H. E. G. PAULUS.—The Life of Jesus, as basis of the History of the Origin of Christianity. Heidelberg, 1828.

K. HASE.—The Life of Jesus. Leipzig, 1875.

Dr FR. STRAUSS.—The Life of Jesus. Tübingen, 1835. The Life of Jesus for the German People. Leipzig, 1874.

A. NEANDER.—The Life of Jesus in its Historical Relations and Development. Hamburg, 1837.

J. KUHN.—The Life of Jesus from a Scientific point of view. Mainz, 1838.

C. H. WEISSE.—Evangelical History, from a Critical and Philosophical point of view. Leipzig, 1838.

JN. HARTMANN.—The Life of Jesus. Historical Treatise according to the Gospels. Stuttgart, 1837-39.

A. RIEGLER.—The Life of Jesus. Critical, Historical, and Practical Exposé. Bamberg, 1843.

J. N. SEPP.—The Life of Jesus. Ratisbonne, 1843. Augsburg, 1862-65.

J. P. LANGE.—The Life of Jesus according to the Gospels. Heidelberg, 1844-47.

J. A. H. EBRARD.—Scientific Criticism of Evangelical History. Frankfurt, 1842.

H. EWALD.—History of Christ and his Time. Göttingen, 1867.

CH. J. BIGGENBARCH.—Lessons on the Life of the Lord Jesus. Bâle, 1858.

D. SCHENKEL.—The Portrait of Jesus. Wiesbaden, 1873. The Portrait of Jesus according to the Apostles and post-apostolical times. Leipzig, 1879.

FR. SCHLEIERMACHER.—The Life of Jesus.

J. LANGEN.—The Last Day of the Life of Jesus. Friburg, 1864.

Th. KEIM.—The Life of Jesus according to the results of actual Science. Zurich, 1882.

F. CLEMENS.—Jesus the Nazarean. Berlin, 1874.

P. SCHEGG.—The Life of Jesus. Friburg, 1874.

NAUMANN.—The Life of Jesus, our Lord and Saviour. Prag, 1875.

E. MARIUS.—The Personality of Jesus in connection with Mythology and the Mysteries of Ancient Peoples. Leipzig, 1879.

B. WEISS.—The Life of Jesus. Berlin, 1882-83.

This list might be lengthened, if the enumeration already extended did not amply justify what has been already said of the incredible activity of religious thought in Germany.

What parallel can we offer with our five faculties of theology and our eighty-nine higher seminaries ?

Philosophy is not treated less abundantly and less liberally than religious science.

Read the announcement of lectures during the summer of 1882, in the faculty of philosophy of Berlin, for instance—more than twenty varied and interesting subjects :—

Critical and literary history.
Philosophy of law.
Logic and theory of knowledge.
History and encyclopedia of philosophical studies.
System of philosophy as an exact science.
Criticism of the principles of Hegel's philosophy.

General history of philosophy.

Comparative mythology.

History of public education in Germany.

History of modern philosophy in relation to the development of modern civilisation.

Explanation of Schopenhauer's world, in relation to
volition and idea.

Principles of ethics among the ancients according to
Aristotle.

Politics and æsthetics of Hegel.

English moral philosophy of the present time.

Explanation of Kant's Criticism of Pure Reason.

Psychology.

What an accumulation!   What a rich heap of
enlightenment!   And what country in the world—
Spain, Italy, England, America—could offer anything
equal to it?

In trying to fathom the youthful mind in Germany, so as to appreciate the state of its religious
belief, I was confronted with the great problem of
the conflict between science and faith—the latter
represented by the Bible, the former by criticism.

It is the famous dilemma of Strauss: either divine
things did not occur as recorded in the Bible, and
then the Bible is no divine book; or they did take
place as stated in the Bible, and then are not divine.[1]

Thanks to the intelligence and the zeal of culti-

---

[1] Strauss, 'Vie de Jésus,' Preface.

vated masters, the problem obtains relative solutions ; and to the public influence of such masters must, I think, be ascribed the persistence of Christian faith among the literate youth of Germany, and the consideration still enjoyed by theology amongst the enlightened. This fact is worthy of notice, if we consider that Germany is not only, like Latin countries, subjected to the attacks of rationalism, but deprived of the principle of religious authority, and delivered over to the dissolving action of Protestantism.

This, in a few words, is what appeared to us to constitute the intellectual life and tendencies of the universities beyond the Rhine.

XIX.

ORGANISATION : CHARACTERISTIC FEATURE OF CONTEMPORARY GERMANY—ITS OBSTACLES—ITS CAUSES—PART PLAYED BY THE UNIVERSITIES IN GERMAN UNITY—NECESSITY OF AGAIN BRINGING ABOUT IN FRANCE THE HARMONY OF MIND—CONDITION OF SUCH HARMONY AND RECONCILIATION OF MINDS —CREATION OF A UNIVERSAL COLLEGE AT THE SUMMIT OF HIGHER EDUCATION.

ONCE again in France, I often looked back to Germany so as to judge it better, seeing it at a distance, through calmer recollections and better considered impressions. Proximity is useful to those who wish to see details, but the *ensemble* is better judged from a distance.

If anybody were to ask me what, in my opinion, is the most salient feature of Germany, I should say, organisation.

For a people, organisation means power and vitality ; whereas a want of organisation means weakness, sometimes decadence and death. In Germany all social forces, religion, science, army, fortune, nobility, seem so arranged as to ensure the greatness

M

of the country. Parties are numerous, in religion as in politics, in theological or philosophical schools as in the Reichstag; but their movements and their struggles do in no wise shake public order: the form of government secures the respect of all, escapes all discussion; and the love of the German Fatherland dominates, and, in case of necessity, silences all discord.

What indomitable vitality does not a country like ours require, a prey to the antagonism of irreconcilable parties competing for power! How is it that, under the blows of the foreigner or the victim of its own dissensions, it does not fall to pieces?

The phenomenon of organisation in Germany is the more worthy of remark, that the country, by its geographical situation, is less predisposed to unity.

Its eastern and southern territories are not strictly delineated: it does not, like ours, possess two oceans and two mountain-ridges as natural frontiers; it is thrown open to invasions and conquests. Conquerors are formed there, and there also invaders can penetrate.

Could Poland ever have been dismembered had it, like Switzerland, been surrounded with lofty mountains? These are not only the cradle of independent races, they are the very ramparts of their independence.

The German race has no more unity than the soil upon which it multiplies; it is grouped in most varied nationalities as regards types and aptitudes, and its spirit is particularist to the extreme. Have those who spoke of unity of race forgotten that the German soil, opened to the four points of the horizon, underwent the infiltration of most divers races—the Latins in the south, the Slavs in the east, and the Tartars in the North?

Despite the preponderance of Protestantism over Catholicism, religion, in Germany, is far from fostering harmony and organisation. In this respect Germany is worse off than most European nations. It does not, like England or Russia, possess a State Church; and Lutheranism, which, under the name of the Evangelical Church, is the form of worship of the majority, is divided into many confessions which are far from being united.

In Germany, Jews are more numerous than anywhere else in the world; they there found a second Fatherland, and they also furnish a powerful element of division. Their progress gives uneasiness to more than one German. Anti-Semitism is often the cause of riots and bloodshed among the German or Slav populations, and only by dint of political skill and firmness does the German Empire succeed in quelling such dissensions. It leaves the Jews free to thrive in finance or in literature, but excludes them from a military career. Many Frenchmen will be surprised to hear that the body of Prussian officers does not number a single Jew.

Language alone does not vary in Germany; and whereas in our country the political power gradually succeeded, from century to century, in blending the various idioms and creating unity of language, the reverse occurred in Germany: unity of tongue was the basis of national ambition, and the pretext of a deferred, and, I believe, fragile political unity.

In spite of all these causes, which precluded its organisation and unity, Germany has achieved both.

What, then, can have brought about a work whose importance and power cannot be denied?

Must we only see in this the result of great victories and of learned intrigues? No. Prussia's militarism and her diplomacy can only explain the mode after which the national unity was brought about: they only explain why such unity was realised under the hegemony of Prussia, and not under that of Austria—under the imperial and non-republican form; but they do not reveal the soul of such unity — that soul which, when independent observers living in the country itself, we feel throbbing everywhere beyond the Rhine.

In closely studying German youth, I soon came to the conclusion that the love of the mother country, the consciousness of its destinies, and the ambition of its future glories, had been chiefly developed in the universities.

In my opinion, the universities were the keystone of the German Empire.

There it was that, in spite of the want of unity in territory, in race, in doctrines, in religion, despite the particularism of the minor States, German patriotism was hatched and reared; there it was that the daring workmen of the glorious though bloody task were trained; there all men of worth in Germany, at the age when Ideal inspires enthusiasm, met to hear and to be moved by the word of the same masters.

The Chancellor's work may fall to pieces, for it does not bear the immortal stamp of justice; but the deep achievement of the universities has a great future before it. Whatever disasters may some day befall Germany, the universities will be to her the ark wherein, during the crisis, her genius will take refuge. Besides, it must be acknowledged that neither the imperial form, nor Alsace and Lorraine, are indispensable to German unity: in this light such unity cannot in any way offend or wound our patriotism.

The more I studied the learned intellectual organ-

isation of Germany, and thus became initiated into
the secret of her national unity, the more convinced
I grew that no country in the world could equal ours
if it had the courage, the virtue, and the science of
self-organisation.

Examine one by one all the elements of modern
civilisation,—labour, wealth, science, military genius,
justice, religion ; compare what they are with our
neighbours and with us : an impartial mind will at
once acknowledge that we have no reason to fear the
comparison.

Nations are not all, in the same degree, predestined to harmony.

The geographical configuration of our territory
illustrates that predestination, and whosoever studies
the French temperament soon notices in it an un-
equalled power of expansion, a craving for fraternal
concord that verges on passion.   Our history testifies
to it, and shows to what remarkable extent we were
meant for unity.   Wherever national harmony exists,
we are in that respect without rival, irresistible.
Our great national, military, political, social, intellectual, literary, or scientific triumphs, all, without
an exception, occurred in the hours of powerful
unity ; whereas the hours of our dissensions and discord always sounded the knell of our reverses, of our
disasters, of our decadence.   Our temperament is, no

doubt, full of vigour, which is noticeable even in our excesses, in our intestine struggles; but we should not too much abuse our energy. It is a game that, in the long-run, will exhaust even the strongest. The time seems to have come when we should think of our pacification, and try to promote it.

It is a patriotic duty, the necessity of which is obvious to every Frenchman who closely studies Germany, and, as I myself endeavoured to do, acquaints himself, in the very heart of the country, with its strength and its ambition.

The first condition to ensure national harmony is to realise it, first of all, in the ruling classes. And as the true rulers of a nation are those who are possessed of the highest culture, it is amongst them that concord is needed. The masses, always passive and docile, will follow their leaders. But how can concord be brought about between people who do not know one another? And, strange to say, Frenchmen do not know one another. Divided into what I will call small Churches, confined in close sects, they sharply wage war against, whilst at the same time unacquainted with, one another. If perchance they meet, it is too late in life, at an age when the forms are, so to speak, ossified, when feelings are cooled down, when, having joined some party, they no longer belong to themselves. I feel convinced that, in order to reconcile themselves with, to always respect and often understand, one another, Frenchmen need only get better mutually acquainted.

On what common ground, then, could reconciliation take place between the cultivated minds who, by their culture itself, are destined to preside over the country's destinies ?

On religious ground ?   Religious unity is broken up.

In a moral or philosophical system ?   The unity of philosophy is still less intact than religious unity.

In politics then ?   It would indeed be futile to expect it: political parties seem enraged with one another.

We must then be content with the aspect of common law, guaranteed by the law itself and by the State in some high institution of higher education.

But it is vainly that we look in the organisation of higher education in France for an institution likely to secure such a concourse of minds.   The general study we made of it proves our assertion superabundantly.   As it is now, our organisation isolates instead of bringing into close contact.

I ask for the complement of that organisation.

The supreme object to be realised would be to assemble in the same establishment the various branches of higher science at present scattered everywhere—to bring together the *élite* of students who cultivate them, and the professors who teach them.

The new institution would offer a twofold advantage : without in any way disturbing the existing system of public instruction, it would in no distant future bring about the harmony, the pacification of minds, national unity.

Why, for instance, not take the *College of France* as the groundwork, enlarge it, and transform it into a *Universal College of France?* Why not teach there the various sciences composing higher education ? They might be grouped into five faculties—

Faculty of religious science.

Faculty of law.

Faculty of medicine.

Faculty of philosophy, comprising literature and natural and mathematical science.

Economical and political faculty, embracing all sciences applied to the development of material and social interests.[1]

The course of studies might occupy four years, at the expiration of which candidates could be required to produce some original work in the form of a thesis to be orally defended.

To provide for the recruiting of the College, why not decree that henceforth none shall be promoted to

---

[1] We are happy to notice, according to official documents, that the reform of higher education, in the sense of *liberty* and *unity*, is now engrossing the attention of Government, as well as that of the superior council of public instruction. See Appendices G, H.

high administrative functions, or be appointed to any
of the chairs of the higher Parisian education, if not
furnished with the diploma of doctor from the Universal College of France ?

In order to let the whole country share in the
advantages of the new institution, every student having spent four years in any faculty could, after a
year's study in the Universal College of France, be
entitled to submit and to defend his thesis.

So as to ensure the freedom of tuition and that of
teachers, to stimulate the progress of science, besides
the official chairs there might be instituted free lectures, the direction of which might, under the control
of the administrators of the College, be intrusted to
any applicant deemed by them worthy of the task,
although the said applicant might have no academic
degree.

The administrative unity of public instruction in
France would thus be left in its entirety, for the
administration of the Universal College would be
intrusted to a council recruited among the titular
professors, under the high control of the Minister.

This simple and cursory sketch is sufficient to
indicate our thoughts, and to mark the degree of
improvement required by our system of public instruction.

What happiness for the country if such a scheme were to enter the brain of some Minister, and to tempt the ambition of a man able to transform projects into decrees !

He would have nothing to destroy, and could complete all.

XX.

PARTICIPATION OF THE CHURCH OF FRANCE IN THE UNIVERSAL
COLLEGE OF FRANCE—ITS ADVANTAGES — PART TO BE
PLAYED BY THE STATE—DUTY OF BEING NEUTRAL—WANT
OF PACIFICATION OF MINDS—GUARANTEE OF SUCCESS FOR
THE NEW INSTITUTION — FEARS AND HOPES — IMMANENT
LOGIC OF THINGS—EPHEMERAL TRIUMPH OF EVIL—MANLY
PATRIOTISM.

IT is to the State (for in it is vested the power of
modifying, transforming, completing our system of
public instruction) that we submit this programme
and our wishes. We should also like to lay them
before public opinion, for, without that, the State is
a power deprived of authority.

How much is it to be wished that Catholic
hierarchy should accept its free place as well as a
brilliant representation of its doctrine in the Universal College of France! What truth most requires is to be known. No doubt religious truth is
not wanting in propaganda in our country: it has
popular catechisms which impart it to childhood,
eloquent apostles who win for it the sympathies of

the people, ardent apologists who brilliantly protect
it against the attacks of sophisms and prejudices;
but, considered as a higher science, it is wanting in
diffusion and publicity.

It remains isolated in its special schools, in its
seminaries. Such a situation procures certain advantages to theology, notably that of being preserved
intact; but it cannot furnish it with the conditions
of normal development. So long as this *régime*
shall last, Catholicism will be unable to expound to
the world the splendour of its doctrine. It will be
known by its worship, its deeds of charity, its hierarchy, its virtues even; but not by its superior
philosophy. It will be difficult for it to enforce
respect from that modern opinion which science
fascinates so much, and to gather round itself minds
of a high culture, which doctrinal splendour alone
can conquer. It will no longer attain those powerful
developments which are stimulated only by great
struggles, and which it only obtained in days already
distant, when in the medieval and renaissance universities it found itself in intimate contact, sometimes
even in conflict, with ever-active human science.

It would not be sufficient for the Church of France
to have its chairs nominally in the Universal College;
it would require those chairs to be surrounded by
numerous students.

It would be the bishops' care to select them in
their respective dioceses. This *élite* of the candidates
for holy orders would form in the Universal College
of France the higher normal school of the clergy.
Thus would be brought about an intercourse so necessary between the men of worldly science and the men
of divine science, both destined to be the guides of
mankind.

There could, besides, be no objection to these young
men living in some boarding-house, and thus being
afforded refuge against the whirlpool of the great city,
enabling them to consult the very sources of any
science without danger to their moral life.

We express these wishes, we sketch these thoughts,
with discretion and respect, not forgetting that our
part is limited to giving expression to wishes which
the Church and its hierarchy alone are empowered
to carry out.

The day when we shall see in France, above our
faculties and our high special schools, a great focus
of universal science, we shall find nothing to envy in
learned Germany. But the scheme in question would
be a dead letter, if, realising at last its high functions,
the State did not once for all give up the doctrinal
attitude it always assumed till now. Its duty, in our
societies so deeply divided in opinions, is to observe a
wise and equitable neutrality, thus ensuring the free

exposition of doctrines. The State is not competent to judge doctrines; but it has the direct mission of ensuring the security of persons.

The University of France made of spiritualist rationalism a sort of orthodoxy, and it was gradually attacked —on the one hand by the Church, on the other by the partisans of more radical doctrines. Hence, without contest, arose the truceless war that was so long waged, and is still raging, between the University and the Church. Hence the discredit that among the public was eventually cast upon the spiritualist doctrines ruling in the University. What has become of Cousin's eclecticism, of the deistical rationalism of our philosophers of twenty years ago? Public education was too often but a tool in the hands of the various sects and parties. Ministerial reforms were not prompted by the progress of universal science, but rather by that of party science. If the idea of State neutrality does not eventually prevail, instead of promoting the union of minds the institutions of public education will be constantly threatened with becoming the instrument of triumph for private opinion and political coterie.

I would cherish better hopes.

Some sort of inherent logic controls the evolution of forces in peoples and in individuals alike. When its time is come, everything must bend before it—the

policy, the material interests, even the soul of nations.
And then, since our country requires pacification, it
will no doubt discover the most likely means of bringing it about.

When we consider the progress of public education
in France, we quickly observe that it was always inspired by some new sentiment, some new passion,
some new idea.

What gave birth to popular education? Democratic passion.

What was the cause of the bifurcation of secondary
studies, as of the creation of those large establishments where science is the ruling sovereign? The
attraction of science kindled in our midst by wonderful discoveries.

What provoked those great struggles of which
education in every degree was the object? Religious
ideas and the passion for liberty.

What most contributed to the giving of such a
privileged part in our programmes to the literary
element? The taste of Frenchmen for external form
and eloquence.

What for the last sixty years has stamped our
public education with such a truly spiritualist character? The natural attraction of our race for the
great philosophy that proclaims human liberty and
the personality of God.

Men to-day seem to be longing anxiously for peace and fraternity. They are tired of their fratricidal struggles : after a century of dissensions and hatred, they at last wish for a truce, for an armistice, for mutual respect of rights. The ardent wish of honest minds is to see science and faith living in harmony, the State and the various Churches upon good terms, and all opinions received with tolerance. Political parties will, I am aware of it, still go on with their agitations ; but, without and above them, would it be so difficult for a Government to close its ears against the clamours of sectarians, to listen to the voice of national conscience, and to become the jealous guardian of the rights of all ?

This sublime end the Government will attain that creates the Universal College of France as the crowning institution of our higher education.

Some will perhaps consider such a college, shelter of all doctrines, as a regular Babel of minds : I myself rather see in it the triumph of the evangelical spirit of liberty and fraternity.

It is certainly idle to expect here below the absolute union of minds. This earth is an arena constantly filled with the formidable noise of human disputes. All we can look for is a mutual respect of feelings, calmly and justly surveying that merciless strife of doctrines. From whom can we expect such manly virtue if not from the *élite* of a country whose first care is liberty, and from a Church whose supreme precept is charity ?

If even parties refused to give up arms, if violent men persisted in obstinately carrying out their fratricidal war to the bitter end, I should still request the creation of the Universal College of France, seeing in it a refuge for minds desirous of seeking calmness in universal science, above the stormy regions wherein fanatics and sectarians devour one another. Thence could be prepared the country's harmony and its greatness.

Let us conclude.

The organisation of our high education is defective. It fatally conduces to division in the intellectual order of things, and, in consequence, in political and social matters. So long as that organisation is left without reform, no progress, no powerful impulse, will ever lead the country into fresh and better ways. Tossed about, a prey to narrow sects and parties, it will lose its strength in internal struggles, and forego great national ambitions, along with the virtues they promote. Mediocrity will pervade everything, and we shall see rising amongst us a generation prosaic and positive, for which " I " means the universe; business, the only aim of activity ; applied utilitarian

science, the last word of culture; wellbeing and
enjoyment, the supreme object of life.

I cannot reconcile myself to such deplorable prospects, nor believe that error and evil will last for
ever. In religion as in politics, in practice as in
theory, their reign is limited. It may sometimes
last over centuries—paganism, Mohammedanism, her-
esies, and schisms, go far to establish it; but some day
or other such reign is terminated. Those institutions
wherein error incarnates itself eventually grow old:
truth alone has the privilege of youth and eternity.

These convictions give us firmness and consolation
in our ephemeral life,—we who die too soon, and
who, fighting against evil and witnessing its triumph,
do not assist in its defeat.

We would hardly, however, understand our duty
were we to rest satisfied with such remote hopes.
We must have enough of courage to point out what
is to be done, when we only have the pen and the
tongue at our disposal; and we must have sufficient
energy to carry it out, despite all impediments,
when we are invested with the necessary authority
and power to do so.

XXI.

PATRIOTISM is more than a passion, more than a virtue—it is the very soul of a people.

When that soul is full of vitality, the people thrive; if it suffer or pine, the people themselves are stricken. It is death that approaches : the exact moment might almost be foretold.

How is it that, with certain nations, patriotism loses its energy and its aim ? how can it be cured and revived ? There is not a Frenchman to-day who does not appreciate the importance of such problems, and who does not, with bitter anguish, ponder and meditate over them.

When we leave our native land to see the life of other peoples, these problems become still more painfully striking. During the whole of my stay in Germany, I constantly endeavoured to ascertain the true state of patriotism with our neighbours, convinced, as I have always been, that I could not have a correct idea of their national life unless I discovered their soul itself.

The first effect of patriotism with a people is its moral unity. //

Patriotism must teach us to prefer ourselves, according to justice, to the foreigner, whoever he may be; to place the country above ourselves, and to sacrifice all for it, that it may become strong, prosperous, glorious.

When at Rome the consuls and the generals, the triumvirs and the duumvirs, applied their genius to the obtention of power, they assuredly placed the Republic above all,—though they placed themselves above the Republic, and the latter died, not for want of individuals, but because there were no more men capable of forgetting and sacrificing themselves in its service.

In Germany, the determined pride with which Germans boast of belonging to the leading race and the first nation in the world struck me less than the abnegation with which they devote themselves to the glory and development of the German Fatherland.

God knows, however, what cruel sacrifices that hard-hearted parent requires from its sons! The most terrible is, no doubt, military service without exception. Many Germans emigrate to escape it. So it may be! I prefer these emigrants who leave their father's roof to those insurgents who, in other countries, remain at home, there to foment dissension and hatred. In withdrawing, one accuses his own want of courage alone, and may yet take away with him the blessings of the native hearth; whereas, though revolted, the other chooses to remain in the country, always an element of discord and dissolution. In this case the famous dilemma, *submit or resign*, finds an application.

In the month of September 1882 I was at Rottweil, in Würtemberg, living in a bourgeois family.

It was about the time of the autumn manœuvres.

A regiment of the Baden cavalry was passing through the little town, where it was about to halt for a day. One of the troopers was billeted in the house where I lived. Nothing more simple, more respectful, more cordial, than the hospitality he received there. As though he were the child of the house, there awaited him fresh water and clean linen—which rather surprised me in a country where cleanliness does not always flourish — and he sat himself at the family table as though he were one of the sons.

I kept looking at the soldier and at our hosts.

Not a word, not the slightest sign of discontent on the part of the hosts : not a complaint on the soldier's lips. Just arrived in a pouring rain, he most unaffectedly told us he had not eaten anything for the last twenty hours. He merely observed that, being a horse-soldier, it did not much matter.

" Horsemen," said he, " eat only half as much as foot-soldiers. It is not unusual for us, during the manœuvres, not to touch anything before two o'clock in the afternoon. Foot-soldiers only have themselves to think of, whereas we must first look to our horses."

This simple fact, borrowed from ordinary life, cannot fail to be of interest to the observer.

What most attracted my attention in Germany was the persistence of ardent patriotism, despite religious division.

I often theoretically had wondered whether a country divided between different and sometimes adverse beliefs could preserve intact its patriotism. The small state of Würtemberg, composed of Catho-

lics and Protestants, illustrates the possibility of such
a thing.   How quiet and patriarchal is Souabe !   At
Tübingen, both faculties of theology, Catholic and
Protestant, live quietly side by side ; the inhabitants'
intercourse is truly fraternal.   I once questioned a
brave Würtembergese on the difficulties and un-
pleasantness likely to arise from the diversity of
creeds.   " There is none of that here," said he ; " we
are all the sons of the German Fatherland.   Do you
wish for an instance of it ?   A few years ago the
Catholics had no place of worship : to obtain the
necessary funds, they organised throughout the whole
world a collection ; the Protestants contributed to it.
To-day the Protestants are repairing their temple,
our old church : they, in turn, are making a collection.   We give to them as freely as they gave to us."

This was neither indifference nor weakness, but
rather the practice of wise tolerance and the fraternal
respect of beliefs.

What would become of that little quiet kingdom,
were the Protestants to apply their power to the
oppression of Catholics ; if the Catholics, become a
boisterous and restless minority, were preoccupied
only with the idea of getting power so as to proscribe
dissenters ; and if the militant Freemasons organised
some educational league in order to oppose Christian
faith as a superstition ?

This would be the reign of discord and the death of patriotism.

A remarkable and extraordinary phenomenon happened in Prussia in connection with the famous *Laws of May*. The persecution that so ruthlessly fell upon the Catholics, chiefly striking at their chiefs, did not alter their patriotism. They remained Germans—Germans to excess ; and on various occasions I was enabled to observe that German Catholics preserve against France the most bitter animosity. What can be the cause of this ? Obviously the anti-religious and intolerant attitude obstinately assumed by our Government, of which, among all nations, it is sadly vain.

Besides, all in Germany, kings and emperors, chancellors and ministers, warriors and literary men, students and working people, all have but one aim— the Fatherland. Their byword is the country above all things. Their patriotism leaves no room for discussion. They do not boast of it as of some glorious title. I am not aware that any German could be suspected of nourishing his ambition on the fortune or the blood of his country.

This social virtue is not, with them, a vague sentiment ; it is a force moving towards some grand and precise object. Such object leaves no one indifferent, it does not shock any belief : it requires

the sacrifice of certain particularisms, the abdication of the military and economical autonomy of
several small states; but its light and its magnetic
power, without distinction of faith or race, attract all
Germans.

Here is the great German unity.

An energetic attraction brings the Germans together, and slowly labours to conglomerate around
the same sceptre, under the same constitution, in
the furtherance of common interests, states, peoples,
races of German tongue. As feudalism in France
was gradually transformed into a monarchy through
the ascendancy obtained by the most powerful of the
barons, so the German confederation was metamor-
phosed into an empire through the pre-eminence
which, by dint of perseverance, ability, political intelligence, and violence, Prussia acquired.

That aspiration for unity stirs to the innermost
recesses of popular conscience. It is the nerve of
patriotism.

No national life is possible for a people, if, at some
time, it be not taken up with the pursuit of some
grand ideal.

Why is England so full of life, so powerful? She
aims at colonising the whole world; she is craving
for the rule of the seas.

Why, despite so many causes of ruin, has Russia

herself a great future before her ? She dreams of
the unity of a vigorous race, the Slavs.

Why, in spite of the revolution brooding within
herself, has Italy grown up to the size of a first-class
kingdom ? She has the passion of unity.

Why does the great Republic beyond the seas, America, astound the Old World by its indomitable activity ?
It has a whole continent to people and to fecundate.

Why, notwithstanding the authority of her traditions, is Austria so anxious, so uncertain, about her
future ? She lacks some great aim. She lost the
hegemony of Germany, and hesitates to become an
oriental power.

Why does Spain struggle in vain in the midst of
internal convulsions ? She has no longer the clear
consciousness of her *rôle*, as a nation, in the European
concert.

Why is France the victim of endless agitations ?
It must, no doubt, be partly attributed to the political, social, and religious transformations of which she
is the theatre ; but still more to the want of some
grand national object that would rally all Frenchmen, whatever the diversity of their opinions and
the antagonism of their interests.

The hegemony in the federation of European
powers was wrenched from France with the integrity
of her territory : since then, her restless activity is

being foolishly spent, at home, in party struggles.
The desire to reconquer our lost provinces could not
prevail against our discords; and we exhaust the
best of our energies in tearing one another to pieces.

I shall never forget my indignation and my anguish on reading in Germany our papers from France.
I often found in the columns of a certain section of
the press more insults against my country than in
the whole of the voluminous Berlin Gazettes.

True national spirit develops itself, in a people,
under the influence of a destiny largely understood.
It is, in fact, but the primitive spirit of the race,
modified in its ideas, its wishes, its passions, its in-
clinations, and its customs, according to the requirements of the aim in view.

If you do away with that aim, national spirit can
no longer be conceived, and the history of a people
remains an enigma. The power or the suppleness
with which they adapted their temperament to their
destiny, is the secret of their successes or of their
reverses. The vanquished were those who, without
the majority knowing it, having ceased to be in profound harmony with their providential end, saw the
decline of their national spirit; the victors, on the
contrary, those with whom that spirit was preserved
in full force. If a man's virtue consists in fashion-
ing himself according to eternal moral law, that of

a people is, under the same law, to be in full conformity with the *rôle* of its ambition.

So long as religious fatalism leaves the wandering masses in the hands of their prophets, and a warlike spirit arms them with irresistible weapons, those masses are a powerful people : they even belong to a civilisation not devoid of grandeur. But when military spirit is failing, when fatalism dwindles away, that enervated civilisation falls to pieces.

Why is the Ottoman Empire suffering from a mortal disease ? Why is it decomposed by powerlessness and senility ? Is it wanting in races, in men, in vigorous and sound blood ? No. It still possesses its proud mountaineers of Anatolia, its robust Armenians, its wild and uncurbed Arabs. But no head seems capacious enough to conceive some new and great aim, no soul warm enough to impart enthusiasm and ensure victory. It is a body without a soul, and which can no longer have one : the corpse is destined to become food for the vultures and the eagles.

It must be acknowledged that, for the last century, Germany has had the merit of giving free and powerful scope to her national spirit. There lies the secret of her fortune.

German unity could not be accomplished without force and violence : it implied on the part of Prussia that policy of ruse and audacity consisting of the skilfully preparing of conflicts, in playing the part of the offended one, and in risking the future in a game of dice with victory.

Mankind follows a path of blood. Murder and violence are mixed with everything—with the evolution of peoples, the expansion of races, the foundation of religions as well as that of empires.

Hence that militarism in Germany, the formidable power of which we have described. It is part of the national spirit; it is even its predominating element. It has been carried on so far that Germany is now but a vast intrenched camp. Every German is a soldier by the sole fact of his being a man, a male and adult child of the German Fatherland.

But what crimes, what passions, what injustices, what hypocrisies, what ruins under the glittering rubric of the country's grandeur!

Bitter revenge, provoked by the first Napoleon's victories, hatched, as a germ, the national spirit in the sands of Brandenburg. Formidable wars nursed it and caused it to come to maturity; and to-day inexorable fate urges Germany on to new and more sanguine struggles.

The aim is not attained: the unity of the German Fatherland is only relative. *Pan-Germanism* cannot rest satisfied with the rule of Northern Germany—it wants all Germans without exception.

Who dares trust to a peaceful policy to realise this colossal unity ? What keen observer does not see Austria eventually and invincibly driven to the south, thrown back to the east towards the Balkans, and, so to speak, expelled from Germany ? Who does not see Russia forced upon annexing all the Slavs of Europe, and doomed to some unavoidable conflict with German policy the day when the Turks, expelled from Europe, shall have crossed the Bosphorus ?

The temple of Janus is not on the eve of being closed in the modern world ; the era of momentous contests seems about to open more threatening than ever. I hope that, in that crossing of swords, my country may still preserve the mighty vigour of her arm, and be possessed by the holy passion of justice.

Though disinterestedness be more common with individuals than with nations, honesty and morality exist for the latter as for the former. The history of a people is not necessarily a tissue of crimes, and national spirit an unruly force. Among all the nations of the world, France is perhaps the only one which, on solemn occasions, honoured her national spirit by her justice and her abnegation. Certain countries found the last word of their glory in a struggle for independence ; the French nation never hesitated to shed the blood of her sons for the triumph of truth and the independence of friendly nations.

Interest, personal interest, exclusive interest : such is the motive that rules the military force of which Germany made the first element of her national spirit.

I never could detect, among the Germans of to-day, even at an age when the mind is most open to chivalrous ideas, the least impulse whose scope was beyond the interests of the Fatherland. Those interests are the unique preoccupation of all Germans. Interest is their ruling law. The great statesmen are but utilitarians of genius. Their selfish policy, more eager for profit than for glory, never, in the country that passively and blindly accepts their oracles, provoked the slightest reprobation.

They make allies, but not friends. Those whom they fetter are only subdued by interest or dread, always fearful of the fate that awaits them. How is it possible not to fear, when placed at the mercy of powers whom justice does not inspire, and when selfish force reigns supreme ?

So long as Germany is animated by such a spirit, will the whole of Europe persist in keeping on a war footing. Men will talk of peace, but everywhere the arsenals will be in full activity, and nations, being placed under the law of the strongest, will be chiefly occupied in threatening and checking one another.

Prussia, mistress of Germany,—Germany armed and preponderant in Europe,—means universal militarism, the reign of dread, of force and interest.

I often tried to discover in Germans some sympathy for other nations. In this object I failed.

The national spirit beyond the Rhine does not cross the frontiers. Germans are never seen to grow fond of another people, sharing its ideas, borrowing its customs, its science, its industry. Always exclusive and positive, they silently, by dint of labour and steadfastness of purpose, imitate what to them appears useful; and in this process, peculiar to German genius, is to be seen a fresh characteristic of the national spirit.

In no other country of Europe is that spirit, soul of the country, cultivated with more care or perseverance. Nowhere do the people apply themselves with a more steady sagacity, and a clearer consciousness of the aim to be reached, to these social and patriotic pedagogics.

It begins in the very schools.

An accomplished woman with whom I once, at Göttingen, was talking about the iniquitous annexation of Alsace and Lorraine, looked at me rather surprised, and, though appreciating my wounded patriotism, did not seem to understand the indignation of my conscience as a just man. " But," said she, " we were from our birth brought up with that idea, not of the annexation, but of the eventual retrocession of Alsace to the mother country. The Alsatians are Germans."

Evidently she knew the patriotic song—

> "The Fatherland extends not only to the Rhine,
>   Where blossoms the vine,
>   But as far as the German tongue is heard,
>   Singing, under the sky, its hymns to God." [1]

It is by means of such insensible action upon the feelings, the memory, and the first dreams of a child, that national spirit is cultivated.

As the child grows up and passes from the school to the gymnasium, and from the gymnasium to the universities, the action becomes more intense ; in the university it reaches its full energy.

The more I studied the *Alma Mater*, the more firmly I grew convinced that, of all the institutions of the empire, it is that which contributes with matchless efficacy to make the German Fatherland. If drill makes the soldier, the university makes the chiefs. In the one the arm is used, in the other

---

[1] *Allgemeines deutsches Commersbuch.* Das deutsche Vaterland, von Ernst-Moritz Arndt.

the head.   In the university, the young man acquaints himself with the genius of his race, enters
in communion with the poets, the scholars, the
thinkers, and all the mighty individualities who are
the highest personification of the Fatherland.   He
learns the history of his ancestors, and hears with
enthusiasm from the lips of his professors the pro-
phecy of the glorious destinies of his race and people :
there it is that plainly the soul of Germany lives,
throbs, grows, and recovers itself.

This was seen in 1813.

When, victorious, Napoleon the First overran Europe and paraded through Germany his thundering
armies, binding the princes of the Rhine Confederation to his audacious fortune, what was the force
that snatched those princes from the fascination and
oppression of the Emperor ?   Patriotism excited in
the universities by the irresistible and fiery words of
the masters.

Fichte, at the time, wound up a lecture on duty
with the following words : " This lecture will be
deferred until the issue of the campaign.   We shall
resume it when our country has recovered its liberty,
or—we shall have fallen dead for the defence of her
freedom ! "

Nationalism surrounds, penetrates, inspires all the
doctrines taught in the various faculties—theology,

law, medicine, philology, literature, history, geography, natural science. All bear the German stamp.

Foreign authors, professors, and geniuses are only mentioned in the appendices; and in their relation with the geniuses, the masters, and the authors of Germany: they are only aliment for that taste for erudition so keen beyond the Rhine. They leave no mark on the intellect. The Germans learn from foreigners, they even imitate them; but they never assimilate their discoveries. Frenchmen, more simple, more impressive, absorb foreign elements with remarkable ease. This is why national education is so much more difficult and delicate in France than in Germany. What young Frenchman does not grow enthusiastic over Kant, Schopenhauer, Hegel even, in philosophy; over Goethe, Schiller, or Lessing, in literature? I never met with any young German taken up with Descartes or Malebranche, with Pascal or Bossuet. Many, it is true, delight in reading old French works; this is but one treasure more added to their erudition.

Thanks to this natural disposition, and to this *pan-Germanism* of education, young Germans leave the school pure, true Germans.

Once entered in public life, the country does not fear to lose them. It incorporates them in the democratic organisation of inexorable militarism.

The German knows that the blood which flows in his veins is his country's, and that he may, at any time, be called upon to shed it for his country.

Associations play a great part in the culture and the preservation of national spirit. In Germany, they are innumerable. Without speaking of those of students, which form the great brotherhood of all the literate men in the country, there are, besides musical associations, those of ex-soldiers, shooting societies, societies of gymnasts, &c. The last-named comprise eighteen clubs, and form the great *deutsche Turnerschaft*, in which more than 200,000 gymnasts are incorporated.

Music, which in Germany is to be met with everywhere, gives expression in these societies to the love of the mother country, and, by giving it harmonious expression, revives and increases it.

Neither has national painting been neglected.

I was struck, at Berlin, with the patriotic import-ance of the gallery created some years ago, and whose foundation dates from the 2d March 1876. It is called the National Gallery. Entrance to it is free. There is not a provincial from Brandenburg or Pomerania that does not go there to see the pictures of his artists. Naturally battle-painting is prevalent. Everywhere are to be seen episodes of the combats fought by Prussia since 1864.

The French dragoons, with their helmets and their horse-hair mane, play therein the great part — of vanquished, of course.

The art is still young—masterpieces are indeed few ; but the love of country, in its anxious exclusiveness, and with its warlike airs, seems to have guided every pencil.

I observed the visitors a great deal more than I admired the artists.   They were mostly peasants and provincial people.   With what native simplicity did they stare at those battles, of doubtful artistic value ! It is thus that the people learn : they must have images, living canvases wherein they find the halo of their victorious chiefs.   A great national painter is a sublime teacher.   Pictures are books which those even who never learned can read ; they, under some striking and popular form, preserve the memory of the heroes, of the brave men who knew how to conquer.

An idea of high national education and of sagacious policy guided the selection of the Prussian collection. No picture is to be found therein likely to shock the simplicity or the innocence of the people ; all are designed to impress upon its conscience the greatness and the love of their country.

As a means of patriotic education must also be mentioned the national *fêtes* in Germany—the anni-

versary of the Emperor's birthday, the birthdays of
kings and princes, as also the commemoration of
great victories.

These *fêtes* mean carousing for the whole population. No brawls, no discordant sound disturbs the
people's mirth. Those I witnessed, often with a
saddened heart, were animated by the most ardent
love of country.

The anniversary of Sedan, which I witnessed at
Augsburg, is still present to my memory : flags and
bunting hanging from every window, people rushing
about in their Sunday clothes, everywhere music and
concerts ; in the square before the church, the funeral
monument raised to the memory of the soldiers killed
in the war of 1870 was totally hidden under wreaths,
laurels, and *immortelles.* " How passionately those
people love their country !" said I to myself, my soul
quite upset.

Thus is German patriotism preserved and developed, enveloping all things, animating every institution, bringing in close contact and unity all the
sons of the German race.

It is important that we should know and take
heed of it.

XXII.

DUTIES OF NATIONS: CONDITIONS OF THEIR NATIONAL LIFE—
DUTIES OF FRANCE: VIGILANCE AND STRENGTH — MILI-
TARISM AND MILITARY SPIRIT—NATIONAL UNITY—MEANS
OF ATTENUATING OUR DISSENSIONS: FIRST MEANS, LIBERTY;
LIBERAL LAWS, LIBERAL CUSTOMS, LIBERAL GOVERNMENT—
NO LIBERTY WITHOUT RELIGION—SECOND MEANS, RELIGIOUS
PACIFICATION—INTERNATIONAL MISSION OF FRANCE, THE
FIRST-BORN OF FREE NATIONS—GERMANY AND FRANCE.

NATIONS, like individuals, have duties to perform;
for if there be such a thing as individual conscience,
there is also a national conscience.

At certain times duties become pressing; fulfilling
them is for nations a question of life or death. The
greatest misfortune is perhaps not so much to violate
as to ignore them. Violation leads to disasters which,
thunderlike, awake slumbering consciences: full of
dismay, people may yet repent and flee. But ignorance brings about the same ruin. Nations pine away
unwarned by their conscience: they die, not knowing why.

It is impossible for a Frenchman to watch the life

of neighbouring nations, of Germany above all—even to follow at a distance the movement of European peoples, the game of their ambitions and of their interests—without being startled, as though some vague danger threatened, and without being alive to patriotic duties.

France has indeed urgent patriotic duties to perform. In the midst of the agitation of all European nations, she has her part to play; in the stormy whirlpool of large agglomerations, whatever the vicissitudes of their destinies, she has her place to keep.

None in the country, rulers or subjects, have the right to withhold themselves from those sacred duties without forfeiture.

Allow me, before closing these pages, having lived away from my country, to state how I understand the duties of manly and vigilant patriotism.

Before all things, let us watch and strengthen ourselves. The law of preservation requires it.

Whatever sympathy our nation may inspire in others, whatever gratitude it may be entitled to, we must not depend either upon sympathy or upon gratitude. Such feelings are no doubt noble, but too fragile, especially in politics, where interest has the first and last word.

Besides, we must not forget that Germany fears us, is jealous of us, and hates us.

She is afraid of us, because, being victorious, she mortally wounded our feelings by mutilating us.

She is jealous of us, because she sees in us the only redoubtable rivals ; and though she may have succeeded in defeating France slumbering and effeminated, she has everything to fear from France watch-' ful and resolute.

She hates us, because she is fully aware that, in the execution of her programme, *pan-Germanism* will fatally meet with still more hostility on the part of France than on that of Russia.

If such feelings were only platonic, we could afford to disdain them ; but they take expression in a whole plan, and in public deeds whose ultimate object is our isolation, the diminution of our prestige, perhaps our dismemberment. Everything which fear, jealousy, and hatred may suggest to a race anxiously watching for its interests, and which cannot be suspected of chivalrous abnegation, German policy practises against France.

For us vigilance and strength are therefore a patriotic duty. Respect for justice is indeed a divine thing,—honour to the great countries which preserve that sacred fire ; but justice requires an energetic arm to defend and to strike, to protect and to avenge.

To watch and arm, when aware of being threatened, are instinctive acts : nations, like individuals, obey this instinct. This is the explanation of the labours accomplished during the last twelve years in our country, to increase our military resources and keep the country ready for any eventuality. What must not be the energy of our national instinct? Never at any time, perhaps, did military spirit grow so cool with us, and never also did we reckon so many troops. But numbers, less than valour, give strength and power to armies; and in spite of our compulsory military service, we should betray our country did we neglect the great art of war, and, misled by vain utopiæ, were we to forget the divine mission of force upon this earth, where justice needs a shield.

We are born knights. It does not become us to take off our cuirass or to shorten our sword. "You are born classical," said the keen-sighted and sceptical Henri Heine, speaking of us,—one of the rare Germans who have understood and loved France—"you know your Olympus. Among the merry divinities that sip up nectar and regale themselves with ambrosia, you perceive a goddess who, in the midst of these sweet leisures, nevertheless always preserves her cuirass, her head covered with a helmet, and a lance in her hand—

"It is the goddess of wisdom."[1]

---

[1] De l'Allemagne.

But, however we may increase the numbers of our soldiers and develop our military spirit, we shall be strong only when we have succeeded in being united in the same national spirit.

Such is the law of unity. As the consciousness of some personal aim is the first condition which, concentrating all the efforts, all the faculties, all the energies of the individual, makes him a powerful being, so the consciousness of a national aim is the first necessity for promoting unity in a nation, and making it invincible.

The consciousness of such an aim seems at the moment wanting in the country.

It is absorbed by problems of internal organisation—painful problems, whose solution is always awaited, and which keep the mind in suspense and in relentless struggle.

Some deprecate democracy, and universal suffrage, its logical consequence; others acclaim both. The majority are in favour of a republican form of government; the others regret monarchy and long for its restoration. The former want to lessen, to circumscribe, perhaps to destroy, religious influence in the country; the latter wish to uphold it. Some are for the Concordate, others for the separation of Church and State. One party aspires to religious and political peace; the other, impatient to see the triumph of

their party, keep up the fray. Some in despair talk
about the end of France—*finis Galliæ*; others, trust-
ing to the end, cannot give up their hopes of a
country that withstood the most fearful trials.

Such have been, during a century, the divisions in
the midst of which France is yet struggling, with the
ardour and the violence characteristic of our impetu-
ous race.

So long as the country is thus distracted, we must
resign ourselves to seeing it anxious, fretful, powerless. It will be deficient in the concentration indispensable to the vitality of a people. When the
hour of appeasement arrives, our country will again
have faith in itself, and pursue the accomplishments
of its destinies.

The most urgent of patriotic duties would then be
to endeavour to attenuate the causes of our internal
struggles.

There is, methinks, but one means of bringing back
peace, and of preparing the solution of the problems
that so much occupy public opinion—liberty.

But liberty having power only when inscribed in
the laws, we must have wisely and thoroughly liberal
views; and as laws are not much without customs,
ours must become liberal also. And lastly, as both
laws and customs find their highest representation
in the Government, the country must have a liberal

Government. If laws have influence over customs, these also possess influence over laws; but the latter enjoy full authority only amongst nations whose chiefs set the example, and are the first to act according to their commands. In the old monarchies, peoples resemble their kings; in democratic societies, the multitude reflects its mandatories.

Such a spirit of liberty does not involve indifference to truth, still less the abdication of personal convictions; it is rather the respect of adversaries, and implies even the highest faith in the intrinsic power of truth. That which succeeds only through human skill is always ephemeral: whatever is supported only by violent passions is always doomed to unforeseen reactions; but that which is based upon conscience and truth, like them is immutable.

Still, I cannot refrain from saying the reign of liberty, understood in that light, will never be possible in France or anywhere else without religion, and Catholicism is the only form of religion likely to exercise its full influence over individuals.

In a country indifferent to religious matters, sectarians have a fine game: boisterous and restless, they will easily succeed in oppressing inert and thoughtless masses, alive only to their own interests. With an irreligious people respect disappears. Where God is insulted, how can we expect man to be honoured?

Is not religion the highest form of conscience ? What law will enforce obedience with a nation whose conscience is not free ?

Thus without religion liberty is not possible.

Let impatient people—those who are incensed at the miseries, the abuses which assail religion—bide their time. Their wrath is useless against those who are no longer animated by the living Spirit of God. Violent men are like wood-fellers, who cut down the tree in order to clip its dead branches.

Besides, the law, equitable law, could control all recalcitrants ; and there is not a patriot, whatever be his creed, his convictions, and his profession, who would refuse to abide by it. Religion would be a paramount motive, for submission to God implies submission to men.

It is thus a lofty obligation for a would-be liberal Government to show in what esteem it holds, I will not say every religion—for religion is susceptible of truth and error, even of falsehood and crime—but true religion, that whose basis is the spiritualism of which French philosophy gave to the modern world the most precise formula ; that whose Christianity is the highest expression, and which found in Catholicism its most perfect social organisation.

In acting thus, a Government would, no doubt, turn against itself many a sectarian, but it would be sure to meet a powerful echo in the heart of the country. What spiritualist could refuse it his adhesion ? And how many sober minds could we find in France heedless of God's name ?

Without this is the fall of French genius, scepticism, interest,—but selfish interest, as ultimate law, positive reason blinded by facts; the death-blow to the ideal, without which no people can flourish.

I am surprised that intelligent republicans have not thought of making that experiment,—that they should not have understood that irreligion never founded anything durable : their patriotism has not been stronger than the vain systems whose yoke they had to bear. Had they loved their country better, their hearts would have been clearer-sighted than their reason.

I dare affirm, that before ten years had elapsed the democracy and the Republic would have rallied minds in unity and peace, had their leaders known how to give all believers legitimate satisfaction,[1]—to open in the soul of the masses those sources of abnegation and sacrifice, of consolation and hope, which Christianity alone possesses, and which no other doctrine or system can ever replace.

Great politicians they be who will pacify conscience, and succeed in teaching the country that simple fact—the identity of liberty and respect.

Modern nations are not simply primitive and savage tribes, whose relations are only those of hostile or friendly proximity; they are the living members of the same civilisation that has succeeded in embracing the whole of mankind, and that sees, above petty private interests, the general progress of the world towards liberty, justice, and truth. A country is great according to the part it takes in this sublime task; and when endeavouring to develop its national spirit, it co-operates more efficaciously in the progress of mankind at large.

Some nations are selfish by temperament and by will, others are generous by vocation and by genius.

Than ours, no country more clearly understood, and pursued with a more ardent enthusiasm, this ideal which dominates human evolution. For the last century, in spite of revolutions at home, of wars abroad, it was constantly possessed with such ideal. France became the most democratic of countries, even under absolute imperial sway; and to-day even, in spite of divisions aggravated by the contention of parties and religious dissensions, nowhere has liberty provoked so much passion. The general interest remains still the main object of our people. It inspires our men of science and our writers, it occupies a place in the combinations of our business men, and even of our statesmen.

P

France cannot and will not live for herself; she wishes to live for others also.

It is her honour to be a humanitarian nation.

This honour is a jewel which no nation, and Prussian Germany less than any other people, could claim from us. It survives all our disasters. France does not only carry it on the point of her victorious sword; it belongs to her genius itself, to her peculiarities of mixed and crossed race. It seems as though our territory were meant by God to be as a select vase in which all mankind had dropped a little of the blood that flows in the veins of its principal races of the North and the South, of the East and the West. Even to our tongue, at the same time so clear, so forcible, so supple—that native tongue of common-sense and universal intelligibility, as it was called by Henri Heine,—that also betrays the predestination of our people for its grand human mission.[1] This view enters so completely into the national conscience, that betimes it leads us to lose sight of our own life, of our patriotic interests. It is the stumbling-block of all generous natures. What blunders, what prodigality, in our European, Asiatic, and American policy, even in this century! There is not a living nation, even Germany, that has not

[1] See Appendix I.

experienced to its advantage French generosity and abnegation.

The idea of humanity should not, however, eclipse that of the mother country; neither should the love of the latter lessen in us that of the family.

Besides, let it be again repeated, the national interests of France mean those of the world at large. In working for herself she works for all.

What a victory would it not be for France if, faithful to the spirit of justice and liberty that moves her, she at last appeared before the modern world as the predestined nation which succeeded in breaking up for ever the yokes, the fetters, the stubborn rule of tyranny!

Let those who startle at the thought of such glory forget their dissidences and come closer together; let them rule noisy and sectarian minorities; let them secure for themselves the respect of all by their equity, their breadth of view, and their tolerance; in a word, let them reign.

Germany has her national pride; let us have ours. Her sword frightens those even whom it protects; let ours inspire confidence in all, weak and strong: the sword of a knight should only be dreaded by oppressors.

To become a free nation, in which individuality

guaranteed by the laws, may enjoy the greatest expansion; to be, in this world, still curbed under so many
servitudes, the first-born among nations,—this is certainly the ideal that most becomes our people, who
raised the most sincere and the loudest cry in favour
of liberty—so loud, indeed, that it shook the earth.

When fondly, like the physician stooping over his
patient and by means of auscultation trying to discover the forces likely to thwart the disease, we
consider our country and examine its national and
moral life, it is impossible not to detect in it many
a proof of vitality and of a future. The hope of true
patriots lays hold of these proofs, which then become
the motive of manly hopes.

The first symptom of life is our indomitable religious faith.

In spite of all the efforts to diminish, and even to
annihilate it, faith resists and still takes root. False
science has not yet succeeded in doing away with the
strong race of believers. Everywhere they still possess vigorous offsets,—among the laity or the clergy,
the ignorant or the scholarly.

Belief in Christ and in His Church is like unto a
fortress invested and assailed. The works of human
defence may here and there be dismantled, and the
engines of terrestrial policy reduced to powerlessness;
but the citadel remains on the divine, unshakable

rock. The ranks of soldiers are thinned down, but the staff of officers is ever increasing; and in the hierarchy of the chiefs no such inviolable and indissoluble unity was ever witnessed. Human science, which placed itself at the service of faith, has grown old; but faith remains young. Political privileges have vanished, often making room for persecution; but in order to live, faith requires liberty, sometimes even trials.

The first treasure of a nation is its religious faith; and France displays sublime stubbornness in the courage shown by great numbers of patriots in preserving the integrity and the honour of such faith.

Germany saw the rise of a new Christian sect: France kept intact the unity of her faith. Politics alone divided Christians; and much is to be expected from the time when, having set aside their divisions, they will meet together in harmony, the forerunner of victory; much is to be hoped from the time when, reconciled, they will, by their moderation, their virtues, and their faith, inspire that sympathy which French opinion never refused to all that is frank, legal, respectful to others, and disinterested.

The great French university corporation, despite its wants, despite its faults—which, in the course of this work, we have had the courage to reveal—has remained the most spiritualist of all the teaching bodies of the various peoples.

None held higher or with a firmer hand the banner of mighty reason. The existence of God, liberty, and immortality have nowhere met with more eloquent defenders. Let some great agitation in favour of faith again lay hold of mankind,—it is not in Germany, not in Spain, not in Italy, not in England, not in America, but in France, that will be found the best evangelical preparation. The great geniuses of Greece —Socrates, Aristotle, and Plato—have met in France their true posterity.

Every people has its national passions.

Two of these are noticeable in France—equality and liberty.

Why refuse them deep sympathy ?

Because of their faults and violence ?

They preserve in the great mass of French people their noble dignity and their generosity.

What hopes are there not latent in these vivacious forces, upon condition of being mutually tempered and better controlled !

Democratic passion would become one of the most powerful stimulants of modern civilisation, if, less strictly equalising, it strove more to exalt and strengthen the humble and the weak, than to lower the strong and the powerful.

The passion of liberty would be one of the glories of our people, if, always respectful of a neighbour's rights, it were subservient to justice, instead of being the agreeable and cringing servant of malcontents who ignore obedience, and a perpetual menace to authorities who cannot enforce their commands.

Democratic passion is equalising in its essence; abandoned to its instincts, without counterpoise, it has a levelling tendency that degenerates into mediocrity. Liberal passion is its brake. On the other hand, liberty is of hierarchical essence, since, allowing full flight to all individualities, it preserves the latter's true rank in the great national life and its true place in natural hierarchy, based not upon arbitrary conventions, but upon merit and virtue.

Such passions are the moral riches of a people.

He whom no passion bestirs may be calm and easy to rule; but such calmness is rather inertia than peace: it is more the sign of pining life than the proof of vitality. Wherever energies, even violence, are seen, we may, by co-ordination, reckon upon great results; but when everything is indolent and indifferent, what hopes can be conceived?

Every force, when uncontrolled, is dreadful. What victims did not the material forces, heat, light, electricity, make before being subdued! Social forces are more terrible still: capital and labour, democratic and liberal passions, not to mention others, will disturb many a century, upset many a State, before they have reached their equilibrium.

We must not curse them, people of little faith, we must cultivate them. We must not suspect them, but courageously try an experiment with them, and believe in their virtue. We must not conceive a bad opinion of peoples who feel the startling effects of those forces; we must rather devote ourselves to them, as to those vigorous children whose indiscipline and errors of youth show their vitality.

It is henceforth idle to look back towards the by-gone times when such passions were still slumbering, just as it would be to regret the days when the forces of nature were still unknown. Our duty is to conform ourselves to the new times, such as, in the course of general evolution, Providence is pleased to send us.

APPENDICES

APPENDIX A.

QUOD FELIX FAUSTUMQUE SIT

AUSPICIIS ET AUCTORITATE

AUGUSTISSIMI AC POTENTISSIMI DOMINI

G U I L E L M I

IMPERATORIS GERMANICI

BORUSSORUM REGIS

RECTORE

E R N E S T O C U R T I U S

PHILOSOPHIÆ DOCTORE PROFESSORE P. O. CET.

vir juvenis ornatissimus

Henricus Didon

Francogallus

Studiosus *philosophiæ*

data dextra iurisiurandi loco legibus magistratibusque academicis fidem, obedientiam, reverentiam pollicitus, numero civium Universitatis Fridericæ Guilelmæ Berolinensis legitime adscriptus est. Cuius rei testes hasce litteras sigillo Universitatis munitas et Rectoris manu subscriptas accepit.

D. Berolini d. *XX* mens. *Maji* anni MDCCCLXXXII.

Curtius.

SEAL

APPENDIX B.

Extract from the 'Deutscher Universitäts Kalender'—22 Ausgabe, Winter-Semester, 1882-83.

STATISTIK DER DEUTSCHEN UNIVERSITÄTEN.

Universitäten	ZAHL DER LEHRER (Winter-Semester 1882-83)						Theologen		ZAHL DER STUDIRENDEN (Sommer-Semester 1882)						
	Ord. Professoren	Ausserordentl. Professoren	Honorar-Professoren Akademiker	Priv.-Doc., Repet., Suppl., Assist.	Sprach- und Exercitien-meister	Gesammtzahl	Evange-lische	Katho-lische	Juristen Came-ral, Forst- bessesse.	Medicin, Chirurg., Pharmaceuten	Philosoph., Philol., Mathe-matiker, etc.	Gesammtzahl der immatric. Hörer	Zum Besuch der Vorlesung berechtigt	Gesammtzahl
I. DEUTSCHES REICH.														
Berlin, Universität	68	71	9	87	6	211	385	—	1063	653	1799	3900	1095	4995
Hochschule f. d. Wiss. des Judenthums	4	—	—	—	—	4	—	—	—	—	—	—	—	~
Bonn	55	26	2	22	5	110	96	61	299	486	419	1061	41	1102
Poppelsdorf	7	11	—	1	—	13	—	—	—	—	88	88	—	88
Braunsberg	7	1	—	1	—	9	—	129	—	—	—	—	—	~
Breslau	55	29	2	30	7	123	108	—	327	352	616	1532	150	1682
Erlangen	36	8	1	12	5	62	278	—	69	141	102	575	—	575
Freiburg	35	9	1	15	5	61	59	41	230	295	152	721	45	766
Giessen	36	10	1	3	4	54	174	—	118	111	147	435	23	473
Göttingen	59	26	1	28	5	119	105	—	191	153	565	1083	13	1096
Greifswald	35	15	1	13	3	66	—	—	57	314	153	659	11	670
Halle	49	23	1	26	8	107	389	—	143	193	652	1377	37	1414
Hamburg	2	—	—	6	—	8	—	—	—	—	—	—	—	~
Heidelberg	44	31	3	21	10	109	46	—	386	207	283	922	18	910
Jena	31	20	9	8	5	73	101	—	116	125	228	570	32	602

Kiel	39	10			18	5	72	66		47	126	142	381	19	399
Königsberg	44	22			19	6	91	126		152	205	380	863	13	876
Leipzig	62	35	11		59	4	171	571		723	502	1312	3111	65	3166
Marburg	47	12		6	15	4	141	103		103	176	381	776	8	784
München	72	8			51	3	33		96	765	619	507	2017	32	2019
Münster	17	4			5	1	42		116			210	326	10	336
Rostock	30	11	1		7	3	104	41		45	53	94	236		236
Strassburg	64	6			25	2	79	69	141	219	183	352	823	26	849
Tübingen	52	6			14	2	79	374	108	412	296	234	1100	14	1114
Wurzburg	39	6		1	21		68			148	534	166	1076	15	1091
II. Schweiz.															
Basel	37	13			22	3	75	66	10	41	85	72	261	63	327
Bern, Universität	42	7	5		27	3	94	36		122	157	52	377	31	408
Bern, Thierarzneischule	3	2					5	18			30		33		33
Genf	57	1			19		77	23		53	108	200	379		379
Lausanne	28	19			5		52	13		35	37	76	171		171
Zürich	37	11		1	42		90			31	183	120	355	36	391
III. Russ. Ostsee-Prov.															
Dorpat	42	2			19	10	73	168		216	595	277	1256	21	1277
IV. Oesterreich.-Ung.															
Czernowitz	22	7			5		34		67	105	189	30	202	49	251
Graz	46	17		1	34	7	101		31	452		58	730	127	457
Innsbruck	39	12			25	1	77		…	…	…	…	…	…	…
Krakau	35	16			28	1	80		…	554	…	…	…	…	…
Lemberg	29	6			17	3	55		323	…	…	134	1011	…	1011
Prag	70	26		2	47	7	150		…	…	…	…	…	…	…
Wien, Universität	80	55			127	8	272		…	…	…	…	…	…	…
Wien, ev.-theol. Facult.	6						6								
Wien, Hchsch. f. Bdncult.	12	14			14	2	32		…	…	…	…	…	…	…
Budapest	61	12			61	6	143		…	…	…	…	…	…	…
Klausenburg	41	1			6	3	51		…	…	…	…	…	…	…

APPENDIX C.

The following is, according to an American scientist,[1] the state of science in Germany, in England, and in France :—

The direction of the scientific movement belongs, for the present, to three countries—Germany, England, and France. The scientific writings of each of these possess a special characteristic and qualities of their own.

Germany takes to-day the lead in the scientific world : at the beginning of the century that part was played by France, but now German influence is greater than French influence ever was.

Students who used to go to Paris go now to Germany, whence they come back imbued with German doctrines, and having but one aim—that of imitating these doctrines and of spreading them.

It is thus they have been diffused through the world, and are being accepted in most European countries. They take the lead in Switzerland, in Russia, in Italy, in Poland, in Belgium, in England, and in the States of America. But in France, in Spain, and Portugal, their influence is hardly felt.

Holland and the Scandinavian States have of late years produced such remarkable works, that their development accompanied rather than followed that of Germany.

Germans have qualities of their own; their researches have a lofty aim, well formed to entice high intellects; their labours bear quite a professional stamp. The German scientific man is above all a searcher. This is required,

[1] Translation of an article written by an American *savant* in the journal 'Science.'

under penalty of losing the scientific rank they occupy, and
which they only owe to their original discoveries. In order
to secure success, they must have made some useful discovery, to do which they must thoroughly know all that
has been done before. Moreover, to surpass all their
fellow *savants*, they cannot afford to neglect any item of
knowledge: they must be possessed of all methods, be
acquainted with all new facts, all improvements. With
very few exceptions, German scientific works all contain
something new and original: every contribution means
scientific progress, not of very great importance, perhaps,
but that still increases the bulk of our knowledge. Do
you wish for a striking and characteristic illustration of
this perfection? Germans who are thoroughly acquainted
with the state of science have a very keen and very judicious perception of the problems which are being discussed,
of the questions to be solved, of the discoveries to be
attempted, of the gaps to be filled up.

They are thus in a fit position to do useful work. And
we know how many scientific attempts have failed for
having been badly conducted.

German scientific writings, though remarkable as regards
the subject they treat, are generally deficient in point of
style and exposition. In spite of some admirable literary
productions, the Germans, as writers, seldom rise above
mediocrity: they are too often, indeed, utterly incapable
of drafting a memoir. Conciseness and clearness are qualities to be acquired by dint of labour; but, as a rule, a
German *savant* little cares about form. He is nearly
always diffuse to excess, and obscure.

This defect is met with, in various degrees, in all the
scientific writers of Germany. Some are satisfied with an
illogical co-ordination; others, among the most esteemed,
drift into the most incredible confusion. Lastly, a curious

and frequent variety of the same defect : if we consult only
the heading of chapters or of paragraphs, a work seems to
be very well arranged ; yet in each of its chapters the
subjects will be found confused, as though some copyist
had amused himself with disposing the documents at
random, under any rubric that offered, without order or
method.

It may be said that, as a rule, German mind is wanting
both in method and clearness. No doubt there are remarkable exceptions. The Germans believe they possess special
dispositions towards philosophy ; they fancy they possess
profound ideas on all subjects. It must be acknowledged
that in this they are quite mistaken, for their minds are
more mystical than deep, more cloudy than vast—and yet
the chief quality of a philosopher is to think clearly.   It
is a fact worthy of remark, though it has been remarked
but little, that Germany has not contributed much to scientific generalisations. She produced neither Linné, nor
Darwin, nor Lyell, nor Lavoisier, nor Descartes—geniuses
whose conquests increased the domain of posterity—and yet
she gave the world great results ; but these results proceed
from the accumulated labours of those searchers.

The German does not understand certain absurdities : for
him they constitute an obstacle and a stumbling-block. See,
for instance, some of Kant's theories.   It would be impossible to make any German *savant* understand them ; you
might as well try to explain to the sun what shadow is.
In a word, German science is but a professional research of
details, which drift but slowly into generalisations.

Very different from this is English science—a science of
amateurs rather than of professors. Some, wrongly, as we
think, will call it insular.   In fact the searcher had not,
until lately, any well-defined place in English social organisation ; scarcely was he received in the universities, where

were wanted only professors able to teach, researches and discoveries being considered but as accessories. The English, their education once finished, leave the universities never to re-enter them. Hence the character noticeable in their productions, which, as a rule, are generally well arranged and in good style; they seldom weary us by the accumulation of their developments.

The main characteristic of English science lies in the taste for generalisations: this is the result of qualities special to 'the nation. A simple teacher draws a general conclusion by a process of individual effort quite different from the democratic method of the Germans, who generalise in bringing together the efforts of all.

Might it not be permitted to say that the English and the Scotch are the Greeks of modern science?

French science is essentially a science quartered in the country; it remains isolated, possesses but an imperfect, uncertain knowledge of what is being done abroad, feels no interest in the original researches made beyond its frontiers.

What a time was required to understand and accept Darwin's theories! although to eliminate from biology the theory of evolution, is equivalent to doing away with the mainspring of a watch. French scientific articles are well written, the subject is well classed, everything perfectly clear. The keenness and the artistic sense of the race freely display themselves therein, but these qualities induce the author to present general views which overstep the aim in view: his taste for artistic arrangement of the subject prompts him to intersperse his work with irksome digressions, principles of trifling interest, facts long ago well known, and something worse still when fancy and imagination are set to work.

Many scientific men hold in certain suspicion French works. This feeling of distrust is increased in presence of

the almost systematic neglect which Frenchmen express for
the researches of the Germans. Such hatred causes the
impartiality of Frenchmen to be suspected in the domain
of science. We do not think that the level of French
science ever stood so low as it now does.

Italy still follows France, but she now learns at the
school of Germany, and her progress is already sensible.

We are convinced that the actual state of French science
will take a turn the day when France shall have resolved
to depart from her voluntary isolation.

Frenchmen stay at home; in the past they travelled
much: let us wish that they may resume their old habits,
and take up once more the intellectual relations they used
to maintain with other countries. France possesses scientific men esteemed throughout the whole world. May
their numbers be rapidly increased!

America hardly contributes to the progress of science by
the number or the importance of her works; compared
with those of Germany they are insignificant. Researches
are not deeply worked out; they do not indeed enjoy the
esteem or the consideration to which they are entitled. In
the United States there are in all but 6000 professors:
in that number hardly 150 active investigators could be
found. The day is still remote when the American professor will have become a searcher.

The severity and the injustice of these appreciations as regards our country have been victoriously
taken up by M. Charles Richet in the ' Revue Scien-
tifique' of November 30, 1883. We do ourselves
the pleasure of quoting the article, as documentary
evidence, in the following appendix.

APPENDIX D.

SCIENCE IN GERMANY AND IN FRANCE.

PARIS, *23d November* 1883.

A week ago we gave the translation of an article first published by an American paper ('Science'), then reproduced by the English paper, 'Nature.' The object of this article was to compare the state of science in France, Germany, and England. This evil-disposed and even unjust appreciation must have appeared rather hard to many of our countrymen.

But our mission is not confined to presenting our readers with praises and congratulations. We must also be informed of what is being said of us beyond our narrow frontiers. The world is not limited by the Pyrenees, the Alps, and the Vosges. There are, near or far, judgments borne about us which, however unpleasant, we must needs be acquainted with.

Children dislike being told certain truths. When told a story, they beg not to be imposed upon. Ostriches, when on the point of being caught by huntsmen, fancy they will escape all danger by hiding their heads in the sands. It is not thus we must act, but rather try to ascertain what is being thought, what is being written, what is being said about us. Our vanity and our patriotism may, perhaps, chafe at such knowledge. But that will matter little if we know how to profit by the advice so sourly given us, and by attacks whose violence knows no bounds.

Silly vanity alone could lead us to ignore the appreciations of foreigners, under the pretence that they are wanting in amenity. It is more useful and more manly to

endeavour to ascertain whether such opinions are well or
ill founded.

Let us then revert to the judgment passed upon us by
the American press. What it says concerning French
scientific men may be summed up in three propositions :—

1. Frenchmen are unacquainted with what is being done
abroad, chiefly in Germany.

2. They do not progress.

3. At no period of its history did ever French science
stand so low as now.

As regards the first reproach, it appears to us peculiarly
unjust. It may have been correct some twenty years ago :
to-day it is quite unfounded. Everywhere in France, and
in all sciences, we study, with increasing ardour, the works
of the English, of the Italians, of the Russians, and, above
all, of the Germans. Never before did French scientific
men bestow so much attention upon the productions of
their German colleagues. The latter's newspapers, books,
reviews, the bulletins and periodicals of their scientific
societies, are analysed, consulted, quoted, &c. Open any
French scientific work that may chance to come across you,
and you will see that most of the authors referred to are
German.

There is, perhaps, some excess in that biographical
wealth. German works, however useful, are rather the
quantity than the quality : that is why our tendency to be
conscientious prompts us to bring to the same level any
small German essay, of no value whatever or nearly so, and
any French work of considerable merit.

Another proof of the interest we take in German works
is the quantity of translations of such works into French.
Their enumeration could hardly be exhausted : the mere
titles of those translated within the last few years only,
would constitute a regular catalogue. The 'Treatise on

Physiological Chemistry,' by Gorup-Besanez; the 'Physiological Chemistry' of M. Hoppe-Seyler; the 'General Physiology' of M. Preyer; the 'Treatise on Zoology,' by M. Clauss; the 'Treatise on Botany' of M. Sachs; the 'Treatise on Physiology' of M. Wundt; the 'Urine,' by Messrs Neubauer & Vogel; the 'Treatise on Physiology,' by M. Hermann; the 'Treatise on Colouring Matters,' by MM. Bolley & Kopp; the 'Practical Hand-book of Essays,' by the same authors; the Treatises on Chemical Analysis, by Fresenius (6th edition), by Post, by Fleicher; the Treatises on Histology, by Frey, by Kölliker; the Treatises on Industrial Chemistry of Wagner, Walkhoff, Balling, Rose, Fittig; the 'History of Physics,' by Poggendorff; the works of M. Helmholtz; the publications of the International Scientific Library (Messrs Helmholtz, Vogel, Rosenthal, Bernstein); the works of M. Haeckel, of M. Büchner; the 'Diseases of Children' of Steiner; 'Mental Diseases,' by M. Griesinger, &c., &c.

We will end here our enumeration. He would possess a fine library indeed, who could bring together all the scientific works translated from German into French within the last six years.

And still we are taunted with taking no account of German works! Might it not be truly said that numbers of such works were not worth translating, and that some among them answer no better purpose than many excellent French works?

No matter: people will still go on saying that we affect systematical partiality or blind ignorance as regards anything but French. Let them talk. A reproach hurts but little when undeserved.

So much for the first reproof. Let us now examine the second.

We are told that we do not produce anything new.

Our writings are devoid of originality. No doubt the American journalist who expressed this opinion never happened to notice a publication with which his director, M. Graham Bell, is perfectly acquainted—the ' Comptes rendus de l'Académie des Sciences.'

If he have any leisure, let him peruse one of these weekly publications, and he will, I expect, feel rather surprised to see such a paper—a regular volume—replete with new facts. Of course, every notice does not refer to first-class discoveries. Such discoveries are scarce : three or four of them are made in a century. Still, the subjects of each notice published in the ' Comptes rendus ' are of themselves truly small discoveries.

Is there in the whole world a publication that can bear any favourable comparison, as regards its abundance of fresh facts, with the ' Comptes rendus de l'Académie des Sciences '? Such is the question I take the liberty of submitting to the readers of ' Science ' and ' Nature.'

I am anxious to come to the general, dreadful, and distressing conclusion, " At no former time was ever French science so low as it now stands."

In order to fully grasp the subject, let us give a few instances.

Among the leading scientific men still living, there are three who will leave behind them a luminous trace—M. de Lesseps, M. J. B. Dumas,[1] M. Pasteur. These are three Frenchmen, three great Frenchmen.[2]

The first named, though he be not an engineer, a *savant* properly speaking, conceived that colossal work, which all believed chimerical and absurd, of uniting two seas, of doing

---

[1] M. J. B. Dumas died at the beginning of 1884.

[2] Numbers of others we could mention, and in every branch of science. But we only quote the names of those whose glory is undeniably superior to that of any other contemporary *savant*.

away with the boundaries erected by nature, of removing an anomaly that prevented free passage from Europe into Asia. Later, he undertook the same grand work for uniting the Atlantic and the Pacific, and alone he did more for civilisation than twenty generations of engineers could have done in all the countries of the civilised world.

M. J. B. Dumas sets chemistry on fresh bases; assembles in a body of doctrine the scattered facts whose law had escaped investigation; points out the relations of atoms and their mutual substitutions; groups simple bodies into series; gives birth to modern chemical science; opens the way in which for the last forty years thousands of *savants* have laboured, walking in the furrow laid out by the master. If M. Dumas cannot, like Lavoisier, boast the glory of having created a science, he so much enlarged the field of chemistry that he has almost become its second initiator.

As regards its origin, that science may therefore be considered doubly French.

As for M. Pasteur, has he not by himself, and by his sole genius, brought about in medical science a revolution such as the course of centuries offers few instances of? The theory of contagion by microscopic beings, of the dissemination of germs, of microbe and vaccine virus, of antiseptics, &c.,—all this triumphant doctrine, which, in spite of powerless criticisms, is daily more widely spread, M. Pasteur alone created it in its entirety. He rigorously set it forth, and, thanks to the strictness both of the experiments and of the demonstrations, it was accepted. There is not a country wherein M. Pasteur's works are not used as guides for investigation. Open any medical paper — German, English, or Italian—almost every line in it illustrates the influence of our glorious countryman. His works, his discoveries, are the universal guides of contemporary medicine.

And this is how French science has reached the last stage of decadence![1]

Is it not truly unjust to talk about the decadence of French science, when among the men of science living at the present day, none anywhere in Europe could stand comparison with these three great men?

Is this all? No. Are we to consider as totally groundless the opinion expressed by *Science*? No. For French science there is a threatening and daily increasing danger.

Though the genius of some French *savants* be superior, though their influence be all-powerful, this is still not sufficient for re-establishing our scientific supremacy of old. We lack *numbers*, and these we must have.

We do not possess a very keen taste for disinterested and abstract studies. The young men who in France devote themselves to scientific careers and work in laboratories are not numerous enough. Science is with us represented by an army well officered, but whose soldiers are rather few. No *savant* gathers around him a numerous group of *disciples* who follow his direction, execute the labours prepared and indicated by him, accept his advice, listen eagerly to his words, imitate his example. The recruiting of the professors of pure science meets daily with greater difficulties.

The reverse is the case in Germany, where in every branch of science the workers are reckoned by legions. Consult their scientific publications, and you will soon per-

---

[1] No doubt Darwin is entitled to matchless glory, and the theory of descent is to-day universally accepted. No doubt also, Mayer gave the mechanical theory of heat. But however great these two men, we have had Lamark, we have had Carnot; no one has the right to ignore their names. We then can claim a share in the triumph of these two admirable theories—natural selection and the equivalence of forces; theories which, so to speak, stand at the very summit of modern science.

ceive that a vast number of important researches have been made by many obscure and unknown persons, diligent and docile young men, *fleissig*, who, having applied themselves to some special investigation within very narrow limits, succeed after more or less time and trouble in effecting work, original and important in some respects. Such work, if it do not leave a very striking mark in the history of science, will nevertheless complete, rectify, improve the data already possessed. In any case it constitutes a progress, however small.

With us a scientific career is, unfortunately, the rare exception. Few young men are fond of studying science for the sake of science alone. As a rule, their chief object is to pass their examinations satisfactorily; and their main care is to find a more fruitful, more lucrative, more agreeable profession than the sole love of truth could procure.

This is the evil from which French science suffers. The public does not understand, does not love science. Democracy dreads it, as it dreads all that is not within the grasp of every understanding. And then, true *savants* become the exception. The *regular savant* is with us an anomaly that tends to disappear. We look upon science in the light of a curiosity, an agreeable pastime. Few men devote to its service the whole of their lives. In Germany it is otherwise.

And why with us these desertions? Why do we profess so much indifference for the grand facts of science? Why have we become utilitarian to such excess? Why also do the Germans have so many pupils destined to scientific pursuits, when we ourselves possess so few?

Whatever the explanation of such a contrast, the conclusion is obvious and inexorable. It is that with us, higher teachers are too parsimoniously endowed. Much has been done for primary education. The schools and

teachers have been well cared for. That is well. But now
the time is come to think at last of laboratories and *savants*,
—of those whose profession is not lucrative, and whose only
care is to enlarge the domain of general science. To such
men must be secured not only food and shelter, but also the
poule au pot and some of the comforts of life.

In Germany the *scientific material* (laboratories, institutions, museums) is infinitely superior to what it is with
us. What else, then, is the question of material if not a
question of budget, and therefore easily soluble? A few
millions more devoted to higher education will raise our
great scientific establishments to the same level with those
beyond the Rhine.

A few millions more. The country must make this
sacrifice. A nation where scientific studies are neglected,
and where high intellectual culture is looked upon as being
a useless luxury,—such a nation, I say, is not far from giving
way to material enjoyment.

Is it wise to admit but immediate interest, and to forego
science under the futile pretence that its profits are but
uncertain and remote? By no means; and it is wrong
calculation to neglect science. It will very soon have its
revenge. In a country where science is considered as superfluous, agriculture, industry, commerce, soon go to ruin.
Who knows if, as a legitimate compensation, science will
not ensure the country's wealth, when the country shall
have made to higher education the requisite sacrifices? It
is not only in conformity with justice that we must take
these steps, it is also in the interest of our own prosperity.

It is more useful to create *savants*, and to give them
daily bread, than to open railways and to dig canals.
And yet we have spent three millions on railways and
waterways.

But it is not enough to reconstitute chairs and laboratories. Something else is required; but unfortunately decrees and orders are in this respect of very little avail. It is difficult to change the morals and the progress of ideas.

What we want is a numerous youth, diligent, hard-working, and applying itself to disinterested scientific investigations.

The love of science is with us the passion of very few men. No doubt these men do their very best to keep up France's glory, and France will never forget them. But their numbers are too small. This is why we must exert ourselves to the utmost so as to swell their ranks.

CHARLES RICHET.

APPENDIX E.

THE TUITION OF PHILOSOPHY IN GERMANY.

Every year, says M. Gabriel Séaille—in an article of which we do not endorse all the views, but which contains some excellent information—the principals of the higher schools (*Gymnasien* and *Realschulen*) of each province assemble to discuss certain pedagogic problems. Each principal represents "the college of the professors" of his school, whose views he interprets. In 1881 the question of the "philosophical propædeutics" was the order of the day of the conference of the principals of the schools of the province of the Rhine. Twenty-eight gymnasiums had sent representatives and forwarded reports drawn after discussion: in order to ascertain the opinion of the German pedagogues, we cannot do better than consult the official account of that meeting. The secretary first complained of the diversity of opinions. "For the last sixty years," said he, "a whole literature has dwelt upon this subject, and one may truly assert that each opinion found a defender." The first question is to decide whether or not philosophical propædeutics are to be kept up in the programmes: out of the twenty-eight representatives of the gymnasiums, twenty-three are in favour of propædeutics—that is, eighty-two per cent. This first point being settled, we must state of what sort those propædeutics are to be. It is chiefly here that the views expressed are widely opposed. Psychology, logic, ethics, metaphysics, æsthetics, history of philosophy,—each of these sciences has its partisans. From the diversity of opinions, the secretary has, however, been able to select certain ideas more generally admitted.

" Philosophical propædeutics are considered as having for their object to bring the pupil who has thought naturally, instinctively, to reflect upon the nature of thought, and to observe that it is submitted to general laws." This aim assigned to the tuition of philosophy shows at the same time, says the secretary, how necessary it is, and what it must be. The object is not to cram the mind with fresh knowledge, but to cause the pupil to reflect upon what he knows, to arrange methodically the ideas acquired by his previous studies.

The question is thus transformed into a more simple problem : Which among philosophical sciences are the more likely to impart to the mind the consciousness of the laws by which it is ruled when it works spontaneously ? To put the question is to solve it. Some of the delegates have accorded much importance to psychology : they maintain that the pupil feels much more interest in it than in logic, and that, by revealing the nature of the mind, it alone made its laws intelligible. But, studied in all its branches, psychology would be a new science ; it would go beyond the subordinate part to be played by propædeutics. Besides, it would raise difficult and dangerous problems : What is the nature of the soul? of its faculties? What are the relations existing between physical and moral things? Psychology must therefore remain empirical, be chiefly studied in its logical parts, and limited to the enumeration of the elements of thought, and of the immutable laws according to which these elements are combined (association of ideas). Nearly everybody agrees to prefer logic to psychology. And this is not without reason : logic forms a whole; and still more so than empirical psychology, by the study of the laws of deductive reasoning and of inductive methods, it enables the pupil to ascertain the laws according to which the mind acts.

What motives can justify the exclusion of the other branches of philosophy? First of all, we must bear in mind that our object is not to acquire fresh knowledge, but to class that which is already acquired. Some delegates are in favour of æsthetics, chiefly as far as concerns literature : science is not advanced enough, it is wanting in uncontested principles. This objection applies with still more truth to metaphysics : let us consider the theories of mechanism, of organism, of space, of time. "Science in an unripe state is not fit for school." As regards the history of philosophy, it does not answer the end in view : it would form a fresh subject of study, and would give propædeutics a part which it cannot be allowed without increasing still the weight which many a pupil is unable to bear.[1] There remains morality. Two of the delegates have energetically

---

[1] A professor in the *Thomasschule* at Leipzig once told me, " Our higher classes are regular lazarettos." If this does not apply to ours in France, it is that, with our system of indoor and competitive education, the best half of the pupils are but ciphers which tuition cannot fatigue, since they pay no attention to it.

advocated the introduction of the tuition of morality in gymnasiums. But objections are not wanting; the following claim peculiar originality. " I had occasion to notice," says one of the delegates, " that, specially with highly gifted natures, moral feeling is very weak, very uncertain, subject to errors ; while, on the contrary, intellectual faculties are fully developed." Conclusion inevitable : ethics do not agree with tuition. Other objections are most specious. There are no such things as philosophical ethics ; there are the ethics of this or that philosophy. But the decisive argument is, that the study of morality is useless and dangerous : useless, since religious tuition is already a teaching of morality ; dangerous, since the professor of philosophy and that of religion might contradict one another, and, thus disturbing the mind, weaken it by scepticism.

The conference of principals sums up its opinion in the following " protocol ":—

1. Philosophical propædeutics must bring to their own consciousness intellectual faculties already long ago brought into exercise, and give the comprehension of their laws and relations. It also serves as a preliminary study to scientific terminology.

2. The teaching of philosophical propædeutics is of absolute necessity in the higher establishments which prepare for academic studies (universities).

3. The tuition of propædeutics must not be accidental; a certain number of hours regularly appointed must be devoted to it. (Some delegates in their reports had proposed not to make of propædeutics a separate branch of tuition ; the professor would have had to call the attention of his pupils to the laws of the mind, in referring to concrete examples : it is really what is now being done in most gymnasiums.)

4. The teaching of propædeutics involves the elements of logic and the chief principles of psychology (empirical).

5. Even within these limits the professor will as much as possible confine fresh knowledge.

6. On the contrary, he will have to take as much advantage as he can of the knowledge already acquired by pupils ; his examples will be drawn from it, and he will thus group and co-ordinate them, and point out their unity.

7. The teacher may, as he thinks fit, indicate some hand-book to his pupils among those which he thinks best (but it is understood that compilations under the teacher's dictation can in no wise be accepted, being looked upon in Germany as irreconcilable with the laws of pedagogics).

8. This tuition will be given in *Unter-Prima* and *Ober-Prima* ; two hours every week for twelve weeks, placed at the beginning of the second half-year.

9. According to the actual organisation of our higher schools, such hours must be taken from those devoted to German tuition.

10. For the full *facultas docendi* in German, the proof of a philosophical education sufficient for the tuition of propædeutics should be required.

We know what the most competent men in Germany think of the teaching of philosophy in gymnasiums. But they have reasons different from our own for thinking so. One of the delegates says, " The study of morality is of too small importance to be admitted in gymnasiums"! Another, whose opinion has already been quoted, utters this monstrous sentence : " Moral conscience being but poorly developed even amongst the best gifted of natures, it is unnecessary to learn ethics." But before giving way to surprise, we must first try to understand. How is it possible to write, " Ethics are not of such importance that they should be studied in gymnasiums"? It is that scholars receive a very high moral tuition; it is because the professor of religion is a professor of morality. One of the delegates writes, "The teaching of morality is useless; it would answer a purpose already provided for; it has not to be introduced, since it already exists." Therefore one readily understands the strange argument which we just now pointed out: its author considers ethics as a science, and, thinking rightly or wrongly that the mind of young men is unfit for such a study, he deems it a waste of time to enforce it. He speaks of morality as a disinterested man,—he treats it as a science. But what is the true reason that philosophy is excluded? Really because it does not agree with the plan of studies in gymnasiums; because it is opposed to their scheme of education. Christianity alone must reign in gymnasiums, it must rule everything. Philosophy is doomed because it admits of discussion; because it means the independence of the mind; because it regards as problems questions which must be considered as indisputable dogmas.

The training of youth in Germany does not only mean cramming into one mind as much knowledge as possible; it also means the training of natural dispositions—the preparing of man for the future. The citizen is foreseen in the scholar, and they bring him up to discipline,—not to external discipline, but to a moral discipline to which he is submitted without his suspecting it, and which, without his being aware of it, must become the essence of his mind. Let, then, those who think that all moral and philosophical teaching is banished from the schools of Germany, be disabused of the idea! This teaching does not only exist in gymnasiums, it exists everywhere—in the *Realschule*, in the *Bürgerschule*, even in the primary school. It is not in a grave and serious country where, teaching youth the disposition of the nervous ganglions of the most obscure of

mollusca, they would avoid telling it what it must think
or do. It may be said that the teaching of philosophy
begins in the lower forms, and is uninterruptedly continued
up to the *Ober-Prima*. The only philosophy taught is
Christian philosophy. Whatever be the private ideas
entertained on this subject, it must be acknowledged that
this *résumé* of the standard thoughts of the philosophers of
antiquity has a high moral value. Do not object that there
is nothing common between this religious teaching and
moral and philosophical teaching. It is given by a professor, not by a minister; it is part of the plan of studies; it
finds its sanction in examinations. It is a regular study,
kept up without being left to individual fancy, but whose
logical and progressive development is foreseen and settled
by programmes. In order to give an idea of what is religious teaching, we cannot do better than translate the
programme of one of the gymnasiums (*Thomasschule* of
Leipzig).[1]

Sexta—3 hours weekly. Biblical records of the Old
Testament (Kurtz Bibl. gesch. 17182). The last fragments
and the verses relating to it are being studied and commented upon (Memoriers to ff. 163). Eight hymns.

Quinta—3 hours. The Life of Jesus up to the Passion.
The second part, with the verses referring to it, are being
learned and commented upon. Seven fresh hymns are
being learned, and those which were learned in the sexta
are being recalled to memory.

Quarta—3 hours. The Passion of Jesus; Progress of
Christianity in the time of the Apostles, according to
Kurtz; Biblical history; eight hymns.

Unter-Tertia—2 hours. General introduction to the
study of the books of the Old and New Testaments—the

[1] Every year the principal must sum up in a published programme what has been done in his school during the year of study.

4th, 5th, and 6th parts are being committed to memory
and commented upon; the hymns previously learned are
being read over again.[1]

Ober-Tertia—2 hours.   History of divine service in
Israel; the Psalms and the Prophets.

Unter-Secunda—2 hours.   The beginnings of the history
of Christianity, according to the Gospel of Saint Matthew.

Ober-Secunda—2 hours.   The history of Christianity
according to the Gospel of Saint John, the Acts of the
Apostles, and the Epistle of Saint Paul.

Unter-Prima—2 hours.   The History of the Christian
Church according to the Apostles.

Ober-Prima—2 hours.   Theory of Faith in the Christian
Church.

Whoever will take the trouble to read and attentively
examine this programme, will soon acknowledge that it is
animated with a logical spirit, and well meant to gradually
bring pupils to the understanding of Christianity.   In the
three lower forms faith is being developed, simple credulity
is being appealed to, morality is being symbolically taught
by legends, precepts become examples, the ·love and the
imitation of Jesus Christ is the full extent of duty.   During the five subsequent years the history of Christianity,
its origins and development, are being studied: thus the
mind penetrates the spirit of religious traditions; to simple
faith efforts are made to add the already intelligent belief,
the historical evidence.   Finally, the last year spent by
scholars in gymnasiums is devoted to imparting their belief
with some intimate and personal reflection.   According to
the idea of Protestantism, the dogma is not an arbitrary
decree that authority imposes upon the mind, but an innermost truth that emerges spontaneously from the depths

---

[1] The indications refer to Kutry's Hand-book, which is in use in
most higher schools.

of religious conscience. Thus with every man takes place
the miracle of Revelation. Prepared by quietude, by faith,
by history, reason must find religious truth as soon as its
own consciousness is awakened.

Thus, *philosophy is not taught in gymnasiums because
there a philosophy is taught.* Young men of twenty are
not thrown into life without moral belief. Instruction is
unanimously regarded as of necessity subordinate to education. Young men, on leaving the gymnasiums, possess
a whole *ensemble* of ideas of life, of man, of his relations
with the world and with God. Of these ideas it is contrived to make moral habits powerful enough to control
and guide youth with almost instinctive sway. I do not
say this aim is always reached, but it is undeniably the
aim in view.

.   .   .   .   .

The writer concludes :—
The men who are actually the leaders of Germany have
a very clear perception of what they mean to do. In the
midst of her preoccupations, Prussia never separated the two
great forces which give power to a people—education and
the army. The school takes the child young and gives him
habits ; of ideas themselves it makes habits almost mechanical, leading man without his being aware of it. Ideas
are man himself ; it is in schools that are being prepared the
citizens of the future and the soldiers of the armies destined
to keep up the conquered supremacy. The object is to
found the unity of the German land by the unity of national
spirit. This end is pursued with a very clear consciousness
of the results to be obtained. A very solid religious tuition
is given ; still no distinction is made between the idea of
Christianity and the idea of the Fatherland : the endeavour
is made to blend religious sentiment with national sentiment ; to strengthen the one by the other. Christian civil-

isation or German civilisation, these two expressions are used as identical; it is thus tried from childhood to exalt, to increase one by the other, two of the most powerful instincts of human life—religious instinct and patriotic instinct. Germany takes up the theory of the ancients : the ancient city possessed its gods, which were its strength and its hope,—gods that belonged but to it. Henceforth Christianity belongs to Germany, and, if we are to believe her, always did belong to her. It was not chance that raised the struggle against the Catholics, that fostered persecution against the Jews,—it is the system that developed its consequences according to spontaneous logic from which we try to escape. Whatever surprises the future may have in store for us, it must be granted that a people which, by education, endeavours to give its own children a uniform conscience, to create among them powerful ideas, and to symbolise in the Fatherland the moral and religious ideas it takes pride in, is likely to become strong. Germany endeavours to preserve her strength by justifying and still increasing it; to succeed in which, she endeavours to rest that material strength on a moral strength, developed and created by religious and national education. It is not here my object to compare our system with that of Germany. I will merely inquire what generation of men we shall have to oppose to the strong generation of Germany, if we bring up our children in prisons where they will be subjected to some brutal discipline, but where they will never hear anything concerning what they owe to their country and to the world. It is urgent, it is most indispensable, that we should start a moral tuition which, in all the forms of our lyceums, of our schools, would have the importance of religious tuition in German schools. France has a morality ; she, moreover, possesses the same faith and ideas : they must find expression ; children must be inculcated with

habits and instincts,—they must be taught to love their
country, by associating in their young minds, with these
habits and these instincts, the idea of superiority and excellence of which France, in this world, ought to be the
symbol. We must pursue this aim with the same conscience and perseverance that the Germans display in the
pursuit of their own.   The philosophical form (*classe de
philosophie*) must not be abolished : in it, however, morality, the history of moral and political ideas, the part played
and to be still played by France in the drama of the
human mind, must all occupy a larger place.

[Extract from ' La Revue Internationale de l'Enseignement.'—
1883.]

_ . ___

APPENDIX F.

SCHOOLS AND FACULTIES.

There are words whose signification seems almost identical, but which nevertheless, when examined a little more
closely, express entirely different ideas, facts, and even
forms, in the progress of our history.

.   .   .   .

We believe we are justified in classing in that group of
words, at first sight synonymous, the two terms *school* and
faculty, often indifferently used to mean the same thing,
but which express two quite different ideas, and which
could not, without seriously altering the fundamental
notions of higher education, be mistaken.

In ordinary conversation we indifferently use the words
school and *faculty* to signify the public establishments in
which instruction is given by professors, who represent and

control higher studies in the special group of science intrusted to them. Thus we speak of the schools of law, of
medicine, of fine arts, of agriculture, &c.; and to distin-
guish this kind of establishment from preparatory schools
of all kinds, we comprise them under the general acceptation of institutions of higher education. These words *higher
education* mark at the same time a line of demarcation
between the schools for higher studies and those of a less
elevated type, such as lyceums, athenæums, gymnasiums.
In appearance these divers denominations seem very clear;
in making use of them people think they perfectly know
what they mean to say : the aim of higher schools is
clearly expressed, and anybody can form an idea of what
we will call the public functions of these large institutions.
They mark the boundary of public education. The young
man who has satisfactorily finished his studies is henceforth abandoned to his own forces : he may, if he choose,
search the science to whose study he devotes himself, enlarge the circle of his knowledge, raise himself up to the
higher spheres, and if he can, if he will, reach the loftiest
summit of science. In a word, the terms *school* and *faculty*
signify those public establishments which mark the limit of
studies and the *début* of a career.

And nevertheless, whatever analogy these two terms may
offer, people would rather hesitate before giving the name
of faculty to schools such as those where agriculture or fine
arts are being taught. Faculty of agriculture, faculty of
fine arts, these words do not sound well. And since the
word seems improper to us, it is only natural that we should
ascertain whether it is not the meaning that precludes the
use of the word. The essence of the thing cannot be the
same, since custom, and even the sentiment of the exact
propriety of the expressions of our language, would consider
as a trespass and violence upon the meaning of words,

to confuse in expression what we often confuse in our
thought.

And this is not a petty grammatical quibble; neither is
it a question of etymology, the explanation of which could
be sought in the history of our language. We are in presence of two entirely different institutions, of two principles
of study quite distinct, and referring to various phases in
the history of our public education. A faculty is not only
a school, and a school is not a faculty. Under these words,
which ordinary conversation too often confuses, are concealed profound discrepancies concerning the plan and the
aim of education, as well as respecting the organisation
and the rights of tuition. These two terms seem, in our
opinion, to sum up the main differences existing between
the University of France, the colleges and universities of
Great Britain, and the United States and German universities. Sometimes language seems to crystallise, so to speak,
in certain words, ideas for which the mind cannot account,
or, at least, which it does not clearly conceive. Attentive
examination of such words is sometimes conducive to a
regular discovery of ideas. Every idea creates, in the
language of science, a fresh word for its use; and when
between words the mind, without carrying identity to its
remotest consequences, finds a certain analogy, it is well
that it should carefully examine the point, and ascertain if
there were not deeply rooted causes that preserved in the
language that which is believed to have disappeared, but
will never disappear. The reason we call the attention of
the readers of the 'Review' to this idea, and why also we
bring together, in order to show their distinction, the two
terms *school* and *faculty*, is that we are convinced that in
France chiefly some advantage can be derived from a little
essay upon the historical and formal sense of these two
words.

But here we meet a question which is precisely the very one that forms the principal object of this study—What, then, is a school? The system of three stages of higher education does not by itself imply schools. The school is a thing that suffices to itself, and is not too difficult to define: it is a public or private institution where instruction is being given; it is the gymnasium of the mind.

There are also three categories of schools — primary, secondary, higher; and it is hardly possible to mistake the signification of these three categories of schools even by adding to them more numerous distinctions, such as higher school of chemistry, of painting, &c. These words are easily understood to mean, not different degrees, but various subjects, of study. Apparently nothing can be more simple. And yet, as we observed, one would not readily make use of the term *faculty* of chemistry, of painting. As soon as we pronounce the word *faculty*, we experience the somewhat confused feeling of something different from that other general expression, *school*. It is true we might simply banish altogether the word *faculty* from the pedagogic dictionary; but Napoleonian codification did not do away with it, but the contrary. It may perhaps be argued that this word only possesses historical importance; still, all political systems of education have preserved it. The word *faculty* must then have a peculiar meaning, and perhaps owing to that meaning itself it survived all political and social revolutions, as well as those in science and education. What is, then, its true sense? And how is it that England does not possess *faculties* but *colleges*, and that Germany, which has so thoroughly reformed its education, has not only kept up the word but the organisation of its ancient faculties, and, at the same time, set up, by their side and on their model, higher schools, without, however, applying the same word of *faculties* to the institutions similar to these in so many respects?

It will perhaps be objected that, in its historical sense, the word *faculty* implies the idea of a teaching corporation similar to German universities. But there are faculties that did not belong to universities, such as, for instance, the faculty of medicine at Montpellier, or the faculty of law at Orleans, when the University of Paris did not teach Roman law.

Besides, German universities of the present day form still regular corporations, and possess faculties in the strictest sense of the word. What is, then, the distinction between a school and a faculty? In order to form a correct idea of the difference that exists between the two, it is important to say a few words about the nature of science, of which the faculty is, as it were, the native land, and the high school the chief application.

It is superfluous to state that no science exists by itself; that all sciences are correlated and developed simultaneously, like the various parts of the same organism, and that the progress of each contributes to the development and progress of all the others. We only call to mind this undeniable truth so as to deduct, as a consequence, that for all the applications of science to human life, it is necessary to possess a previous *ensemble* of knowledge relating to each of them. Whoever embraces a career is obliged to acquire the knowledge and the limit where, if we may say so, the province of his scientific education will at first be defined, not by the idea of science in itself, but by the requirements of the career he wishes to embrace, such as jurisprudence, medicine, philology, theology. Besides, these sciences and branches of knowledge may very well exist by themselves: jurisprudence does not require theology, nor medicine philology; and every one of these sciences may be conceived as forming a whole, while its various parts are being developed and begin to create special sciences. It is thus only natural that, at the outset of the preliminary tuition of a vocation (*Berufsbildung*), education be limited to an *ensemble* of knowledge of a double nature : on the one hand, all the special branches contained in the whole of every science, with their special progress; on the other hand, special sciences themselves, considered outside of all logical and philosophical unity, according to the nature and the particular wants of each vocation. It is easy to form teaching bodies for each of these sciences of vocation (*Berufswissenschaften*) that will involve all the special branches of that science special in itself—such as, for instance, civil law, criminal law, and the law of nations for jurisprudence.

If, then, any calling whatsoever, like that of a judge, require special instruction for the discharge of public functions, it will at first sight be sufficient to expect from the future magistrate but that special instruction acquired by him in view of his vocation—jurisprudence ; that is, civil law, criminal law, the law of nations. It would, then, be idle to organise an *ensemble* of tuition, in some measure disinterested, and only related to one another by a mere philosophical tie ; it would be far wiser to take into account only special vocations, and the practical aim which, for instance, the jurisconsult has in view. It seems as though society would be perfectly satisfied with tuition understood in this light. And these institutions, limited to their practical object—living, so to speak, their own life, having no contact with the other sciences, satisfied to go deeply into the special object of their studies useful to life, foreign to the doubts that assail those who investigate scientific ideas outside their curriculum,—these institutions are the *higher schools.*

It is therefore easy to understand that a good system of

tuition may be devised by the means of as many higher schools as there are, we will not say ideal parts of a logical system of sciences, but careers useful to society and to the practical wants of existence. And, in fact, with all civilised peoples, there will be as many such higher schools as there will be leading vocations acknowledged as indispensable by society. This is what explains the existence of higher schools of agriculture, of music, by the side of the schools of jurisprudence and medicine. These high schools meet imperious social wants. Still they are not scientific institutions. And, this distinction once admitted, it must be acknowledged that in these schools, at least in principle, it is less a question of science, of the great unity of knowledge, of the σοφία of the Greeks, than of the practical and honourable applications of what these same Greeks termed the τέχναι, the arts, the liberal arts (to make use of a medieval expression, these in the middle ages being sometimes classed with handicrafts).

And judging these high schools from the standpoint of primary, secondary, and higher education, such higher education would involve the whole of higher schools, for which secondary education would form a sort of preliminary stage (*Vorbildung*); so that, as in France, the university would comprise the whole system of higher and secondary schools organised and hierarchised according to the same principles and under the same administrative control. Each science would then possess its organisation, its lectures, its professors, its examinations,—the whole of this in view of a special career. Could not an organisation of this nature suffice for both the development of the human mind and the necessities of practical life?

In the middle ages there were high schools of jurisprudence and medicine in several parts of Europe, in Italy as well as in France ; but we see everywhere, at the same time, a movement of centralisation that tended to group the various schools in a certain unity, misunderstood at first, quite formal, and without any really scientific tie, but that succeeded in securing all the forces of such unity, in giving birth to its organisation, to its rights, in appointing its ruler, under the name of university. It is true that in the beginning, and even after several centuries, men experienced great trouble in giving a correct idea of a university. Boullaye, in his 'Histoire de l'Université de Paris,' furnishes frequent proofs of it in the thirteenth and fourteenth centuries; and we also possess the historical proof that, in the sixteenth century, in Germany, they could not at all account for the nature and the special function of a university, or for the difference existing between academies, lyceums, gymnasiums, and universities. We thus read, in 1502, in the statutes which the Emperor Maximilian gave the University of Wittemberg, since then so famous by the reform that it gave birth to,—"Ut studium generale sive universitatem, aut gymnasium institueremus." Maximilian II., in the statutes of the University of Helmstadt (1579), said,—"Privilegiis et immunitatibus studii universalis seu gymnasii." The privilege of the University of Halle contains the following words,— " Tale sublimius gymnasium sive academiam ; " and that of Göttingen,—"Sublimius gymnasium sive academiam et studium universale," &c. The first writer who tried to define the true nature and meaning of a university, compared with academies and lyceums, is, to the best of our knowledge, Meiners, one of the celebrities of the University of Göttingen, who, towards the close of the last century, published a work " on the constitution and administration of higher schools," and, a short time afterwards, a ' History of the Foundation and Progress of Higher Schools,' four volumes (1802). But he did not fully grasp the nature of

universities : for him, their characteristic feature lies solely
in their co-operative element, in their constitution, their
jurisdiction, their privileges, their rights of conferring
scientific degrees ; whereas, in the very words that recite
their ancient privileges, he ought to have read the proof
that the nature of these universities proceeded chiefly from
the *studium generale* at Paris, Padua, Vienna, Prague, &c.,
and that the organisation and the privileges of these great
corporations were indeed but the consequence of their
functions, that led them to bring together in a body, as
studium generale, all the studies of higher schools, to meet
the unity claimed by the *ensemble* of sciences,—a union
that justifies for each university the glorious title of *Alma
Mater*.

What was to be understood by these words—general
or more sublime study ? Was it something else than the
particular study of separate sciences in the high schools
extant ? Could these universities add any fresh knowledge
to that already taught in the special schools ? Could, for
instance, the University of Paris cultivate Roman law better
than the high school of law at Orleans, or medicine more
successfully than Montpellier ? And yet it was felt that
there was something more grand and more vivifying in the
unity of those higher schools, with their professors, masters,
bachelors, and licentiates. The universities attracted the
high schools, they blended them into one body : the latter
renounced their independent existence by incorporating
themselves with the university whole ; their discipline, as
well as their organisation, became an integral part of the
university, and in that union they lost the name of *school*
to take that of *faculty*. We know this is the history of the
formation of faculties ; and we again inquire, Where lies
the great principle that brought about that transformation—
as also, for what motive, in the midst of the modern organ-

isation of education in Europe, we preserve the name and the idea of an institution, which, at first sight, only possesses a historical right to exist in a civilisation that has developed sciences and their tuition in a measure of which bygone centuries had certainly no idea?

And yet it does not seem very difficult to us to show precisely the nature of high schools compared with the faculties, which were mostly but high schools joined to a university.

We now hope it will be easy to find the true sense of the great difference which, in our opinion, exists between a higher school and a faculty. Every higher school is limited by its discipline and its object, and it does not concern itself with anything beyond these limits: we thus say that all superior instruction in higher schools is, by its nature, a practical teaching. On the other hand, every faculty, though containing in its instruction all that a higher school offers to its pupils, claims by its nature a study of philosophy and general history, and theoretical conception as the complement of practical discipline. The higher schools lead always to experiments, whereas the faculty leads to systems. The former gives what is necessary for social life; the latter, though ensuring the same advantage, requires every vocation to have a point in which it rises above those narrow limits which immediate utility ascribes to it. The higher school is satisfied with laying before its pupils that which is certain; the faculty teaches its disciples to search and to comprehend that which is true. The higher school dismisses its pupils when they have learned all they require; the faculty insists upon their learning also that of which they may never have to make a direct application. If the value of a higher school consists in practical knowledge, that of a faculty lies in the conception of the unity of all human knowledge and discipline. Both follow a system often the same; but the system of a higher school is limited by its practical object, whereas that of a faculty considers each actual state of a practical system as being part of a whole belonging to the development of the general civilisation of mankind. And this is why the organisation of higher schools has a character distinguishing it from that of faculties—character that reappears, so to speak, by the innate force of things, and which sometimes subsists without our being aware of it. We may found as many higher schools as we please; every one of them will take its name from its special object, and the organisation of its studies and of its discipline may be quite the same as that of faculties. But these higher schools do not require to be united in a common teaching body,— every one of them may and can exist for itself; it suffices to itself, because its function is filled by its object and its aim. But it is impossible that a faculty could exist isolated from other faculties, because in giving all a higher school can and intends to teach, the faculty expects besides from its students a study at least elementary of philosophy and general history. If the higher school is the teaching of nature, of special forces and their object, the faculty presents a scientific teaching based, at the same time, upon all sciences. A faculty is unable to exist for itself; it still contains precisely what the ancient statutes of the universities meant by the words *studium generale, studium sublimius*. So soon as faculties sprang up, they blended themselves in the unity of some great body, where high disciplines are not only in juxtaposition, but where they rise to the dignity of science by philosophical and historical studies; and so soon as such union takes place in a body common to all sciences, the great principle of the division of labour becomes obvious. Each group of studies becomes a faculty, and the faculty of philosophy becomes distinct from that of theology, the faculty of law is separated from that of medicine.

Thus were born the four faculties, and it is not legislation or administration of public instruction,—whatever it may be, it is the superior force of things, or rather, the nature of the life of the mind itself,—which created that system of faculties—faculties which, by their union in a common body, and by the powerful unity that history and philosophy stamp upon the tuition of all sciences, became a *university.* This is why higher schools do not, and never will, form a university; whereas, as already seen, faculties cannot exist outside of a university. And this explains why the difference is so great between higher schools, although they may bear the same name, whereas universities are all alike; and the innate difference between the faculties and the higher schools is so great, that it alone suffices to enable us to understand why language and literature, and even legislation and administration, do not feel themselves free to apply the name of the one to the organisation of the other. It is impossible, or rather it would sound very odd, to speak of a faculty of painting, of agriculture, even of chemistry or literature; whereas even the most systematic of legislation on public instruction, French legislation, could not entirely do away with the word faculty for the great groups of science. This was the starting-point of our observations; I think it is as well that we laid them before our readers: and if the notion of science be clear, that of faculty, distinct from the idea of higher school, will none the less be so.

Nevertheless, we confess our observations are somewhat rather abstract. The union of faculties by the unity of sciences in a university is an organic, and, at the same time, historical fact; but if we are to deduct from this fact practical consequences for the organisation of education, this fact itself must not only exist, but also be brought into exercise : if not, the distinction between *faculty* and *school* must remain, like the idea of faculty and that of university itself, a theoretically highly interesting conception, though of no application in practice. We have, then, a right to inquire how and under what form it was enabled to impose itself upon the great system of education.

We must take care not to overstep the limits of an essay, which, perhaps, is already too long. We will, then, confine ourselves to saying that it is history itself which gave the answer to this question, and that the public law of university tuition in Germany, as in Austria and in Scandinavia, has, from the beginning of our society, formulated this answer in the positive order of studies and the examinations of universities. However true and beautiful may appear the theory of faculty and university, the ancient *studium sublimius* cannot be left to the fancy of students. The greater number of these study science in view of some special career, and care little about philosophy and history, —and, if it were not for the system of examinations, the philosophical faculty, with all its laboratories and its lectures, would perhaps be deserted by most students. This the university system has well understood : it never was willing to leave science to the mercy of young men, and compel them only to the study of positive discipline. Thus the general rule is that every student, during the eight half-years of his studies, must attend at least one course of lectures on philosophy and one on history, and that his studies are not considered as complete if he fail to enter his name for these two courses of lectures. On the other hand, it is also this nature of faculties which gave birth throughout Germany to the system of examinations. These are divided into two groups—theoretical and practical. The theoretical examination follows university studies, and requires not only a certain knowledge of philosophical ideas, relating chiefly to the various phases of the history of philosophy, but also historical notions, mainly in the history of the special branch of study relating to the profession to which the student intends devoting himself. It is true that medicine is an exception, and that the examination of medical students, upon their leaving the university, is, at the same time, practical and theoretical; but the other faculties always insist upon the elements of philosophical and historical notions, and they are sometimes rather severe in this respect.

This university or theoretical examination is, throughout Germany as in Austria, followed by a practical examination, but which only takes place at the end of a few years, after the introduction of the young man into practice. It is only then that candidates are expected to be conversant with all the positive and practical notions which theologians, barristers, and functionaries need to be acquainted with. And since the university examination is the preliminary condition of being allowed to go up for the practical subsequent examination, young men are bound, at least within certain limits, to attend the philosophical and historical lectures, and they would hardly dare appear before any examining board without possessing at least some pretty complete notion of these elements of a university education. The great difference between the scientific education of Germany and that of the other countries of Europe lies precisely in the fact that every educated young man brings away with him from the university at least a general idea of science, besides the positive knowledge necessary for the career he is about to embrace; and if he has not learnt many things beyond the limits of his special instruction, he, at least, is enabled to learn that even of which he has no material need, and even to respect a little that which he has not understood. And this is why he loves his university, because the impression it imparts to his youthful mind, the development of his ideas beyond the limits of his professional knowledge,—all these constitute so many recollections that are always present to his mind: they are the great ties that unite him in communion of ideas with the general life of the past as well as with the eternal labour of the human mind: he looks upon them as priceless treasures that keep him company even in the loneliness of an existence that at times is despairingly empty.

And to wind up these theoretical observations by a very practical one for positive studies themselves, we must point out that the serious consequence of this principle of university tuition in faculties as compared with higher schools is, that philosophy and history being, in the former, integral parts of higher education, become themselves studies of vocation (professional studies). There is a thing, a force, with which, at momentous periods, human life cannot dispense without feeling the want of an essential element, upon which depends sometimes the last success, and from which proceeds the power of combating indifference and egotism, those two enemies of all that is grand and beautiful: it is ideal. And history and philosophy are the sources of that force: alone, ideal never forsakes us ; we must give it as a friend and inseparable companion to youthful minds still capable of understanding the value of that which has ceased to be useful.

Dr Lorenz de Stein,
Professor in the Vienna University.

[Extract from the ' Revue Internationale de l'Enseignement.'—
1882. Masson.]

APPENDIX G.

ORGANISATION OF HIGHER EDUCATION.

Before leaving the Ministry of Public Instruction to take the Portfolio of Foreign Affairs, M. Jules Ferry sent to the various rectors of the University the following important circular note, respecting the organisation of higher education :—

MONSIEUR LE RECTEUR,—

The various measures which, for the last five years, I have been taking concerning the faculties, were amply sufficient to evince the paramount importance I ascribe to all that is likely to foster in higher education the sentiment of responsibility, the habit of self-rule. We should have attained a great result indeed if we could some day constitute universities bringing together the most varied teachings that they might reciprocally help one another, administering themselves their own affairs, appreciating fully their duties and their mission, inspiring themselves with the ideas peculiar to each part of France within the limits required by the unity of our country, competing with neighbouring universities, associating in their rivalry the interest of their own prosperity with the desire of great cities to surpass one another, and thus acquiring special merits and titles to honour. I do not forget that time is necessary to ensure such achievements ; that, in such undertakings, however legitimate the ambition, nothing must be done with precipitation or left to hazard. I think, however, considering the results we have already obtained, that the question may at least be investigated.

On so serious a subject, as in all others, it is chiefly from the opinion, the enlightenment, and the abnegation of the teaching body, that real progress is to be expected : I therefore deem it necessary to invite it to expose the views it holds in this respect. It is idle to state that no restriction whatsoever is to be opposed to free expression in the discussions about to be opened first of all in the faculties, in higher and preparatory schools, then in academic councils.

The subject is important enough that plenty of time should be given to think it over. It will be sufficient that the deliberations of the faculties be submitted before academic councils in the July session. If even a further delay should appear necessary, every advantage is to be derived from its being granted ; the main object is to secure profound and conscientious investigation.

I will refer to a set of questions which, I think, ought to be studied, and which I desire the faculties to discuss in turn, so that it may be easier to sum up, and to compare the opinions expressed. The faculties may, of course, afterwards examine any other questions they may deem worthy of interest.

1. *Of Universities.*—Would there be any advantage in grouping the various faculties of the same academic jurisdiction into a university ? What services would such a measure be likely to render ?

2. What kind of autonomy would be desirable for each faculty in the university ?

3. What should be the administrative mode of these universities ? Should there be a council composed of the deans (*doyens*) and of an annual delegate elected by each faculty ? Should such council be recruited on different principles ?

4. Should the dean be elected ? Should his appoint-

ment be annual ? Could any advantage accrue from adopt-
ing other rules ?

5. What should be the attributions of the university
council ? Its scientific and its administrative attributions ?

6. Who should be the head of the university ? What
do you think of a head yearly elected as president of the
university ? Or what other title could be given ? What
should the president's attributions be ? What part should
he play towards the council ?

7. Attributions of the annual rector representing the
central authority ?

8. What part of the actual revenue of faculties should
be placed entirely at the disposal of the university ? Is it
desirable that universities should have a yearly endowment,
calculated according to the mean revenue of faculties, in
each academic centre, during the last five years ?

9. Are you of opinion that civil personality granted to
faculties would ensure to them important advantages, by
making endowments more easily feasible, and urging all
municipalities to consider universities as institutions to
the prosperity of which they should contribute ?

10. What should be the maximum and the minimum of
State rights ?

11. What are the best means likely to develop in universities the life and the spirit of progress ?

The deliberative bodies are invited to sum up their views
in the way generally adopted for projects of laws and
decrees.

The constitution of universities administering themselves
under the high control of the State is no doubt an ideal
that we must endeavour to attain; still, it is important to
take into account public spirit, the past history of our
country, the different customs noticeable in the divers
faculties, some already ancient traditions existing among

the professors and admitted by the public opinion. Our only preoccupation must be to secure serious and real progress, easy to be obtained by simple and practical means. We have not the right to attempt experiments whose issue might be doubtful : should the least uncertainty strike the faculties regarding the success of the reforms I submit to their notice, it is their duty to say so. To put off a reform, is often, for the minds whose sole object is public boon, the best means of ensuring their easy and complete triumph some years later.

You will be good enough, in summing up the various views expressed to you, to give me your own personal opinion.

Receive, Monsieur le Recteur, the assurance of my most distinguished consideration.

The President of the Council,
Minister of Public Instruction and Fine Arts,
JULES FERRY.

APPENDIX H.

DECREE OF THE 24TH JULY, AUTHORISING FREE LECTURES IN FACULTIES.

THE PRESIDENT OF THE FRENCH REPUBLIC,

Considering the report of the President of the Council, Minister of Public Instruction and Fine Arts ;

Having heard the Superior Council of Public Instruction,

DECREES :—

Article 1.—Free lectures may be delivered in faculties by professors not belonging to the staff of such faculties.

Article 2.—Any doctor of letters or of sciences may be authorised to deliver, in the State faculties, free lectures upon the subjects corresponding with the order of studies for which he has been appointed a doctor.

Such authorisation is granted by the Secretary of State, upon the proposal or advice of the faculty in which the lectures are to take place, and upon a special report from the rector.

The professors in the various State establishments of higher education, the correspondents or members of the Institute, are considered as belonging to the body of doctors.

Article 3.—The same authorisation may, according to favourable advice from the faculty, be granted to persons unprovided with the degree of doctor, in case of their having specially studied the matters upon which they intend to lecture.

Article 4.—In any case, the authorisation will only be valid for one year.

It may be renewed according to the conditions set forth in Articles 2 and 3.

Upon the advice or proposal of the faculty, the Minister may always withdraw it.

Article 5.—The bill relating to free lectures can only be posted by the orders of the faculty.

As regards surveillance and discipline, free lectures are assimilated to the lectures of the faculty.

Article 6.—The free lectures are either public or private. When public, admission to them is submitted to the same conditions as for the lectures of the faculty.

No person can be admitted to the private lectures without the assent of the professor. Any member of the faculty or of the academic administration may, however, at any time, attend the free lectures, even when private.

Article 7.—The expenses arising from free lectures are to be charged to the professor; they are to be settled by mutual agreement between the dean and the professor, under the approbation of the rector.

The authorisation for delivering free lectures does not involve the use of instruments, apparatus, &c., or the employment of the staff belonging to the faculty.

Article 8.—Private free lecturers may charge a certain fee payable by students, for the benefit of the professor.

Article 9.—Free lectures may be annual, half-yearly, or quarterly; they must number at least ten lectures every quarter.

Faculties of Medicine.

Article 10.—The free lectures in the faculty of medicine of Paris are still subjected to the prescriptions contained in the Presidential decision of 9th February 1881.

Every faculty of medicine and every higher school of pharmacy shall submit to the approval of the Minister a set of regulations relative to free lectures.

Faculties of Law.

Article 11.—The above decree may, by ministerial decision, be applied to faculties of law, at their request.

Article 12.—The President of the Council, Minister of Public Instruction and Fine Arts, is intrusted with the execution of the present decree.

JULES GRÉVY.

By the President of the Republic:

The President of the Council,
Minister of Public Instruction and Fine Arts,

JULES FERRY.

APPENDIX I.

In 1784 the following subject was given as competition by the academy of Berlin : " Of the causes of the universality of the French language." Rivarol sent in an essay; his speech had the greatest success before the academy and in Paris : but it is not generally known that he only obtained half the prize, this being shared with a German scholar, M. Schwab, secretary to the Duke of Würtemberg. Rivarol's speech was not free from defects : there is too much rhetoric in the preamble; the last page is emphatic; besides, we could take up in the whole speech many a passage of bad taste, thoughtless assertions upon history and the origin of languages, allusions full of affectation. Still, through this display of bad academic style some pages subsist that bear the stamp of the writer and thinker.

The author is aware that the proud privilege of universality devolved upon the French tongue is owing to intricate and delicate causes : it is the situation of France, her political constitution, the influence of her climate, the genius of her writers, the character of her inhabitants, and the high opinion of herself which she enforced upon the world. The chief idea is that the character of nations and the genius of their tongue follow in the same steps, and that it is the admirable property of speech thus to unveil man in his entirety. The genius of a language arises from numerous causes, among which are to be noticed the sweetness or the harshness of articulations, the abundance or the scarcity of vowels, the prosody and the length of words, their filiations—lastly, the number and the form of structures they take in their combinations. These causes are intimately united to the climate and the character of each people in particular; the union of the character of a people and of the genius of its tongue is based upon the eternal covenant of speech and thought.

The chief distinction between our tongue and ancient and modern languages lies in the order and structure of the sentence. This order must always be direct: a Frenchman will always name first the *subject* of the sentence, then the *verb*—that is, the action—and lastly, the *object* of that action. This is logic natural to all men, this constitutes common-sense. Now this method is nearly always contrary to sensations which name the object first. This is why all peoples who gave up the direct method had recourse to inversions. But what traps, what surprises, what obscurity, what artifice and withering of the idea, in inverted languages! Frenchmen remained faithful to the logical order, as though it were reason itself; French syntax is incorruptible. That which is not clear cannot be French. This is why, despite the richness and the beauty of its poetry, it is owing to its prose that the French tongue has reigned, reigns, and will ever reign. Prose unveils the nudity of thought; with it no weakness can be tolerated. Our language is, then, the natural expression of a people that received the impressions of all the peoples of Europe, that placed taste in moderate opinions, and of which it may be said that its books compose the library of mankind.

Such is the substance of Rivarol's speech, made a little clearer and more methodical, it must be acknowledged, by the brilliant analysis of M. Caro. What the laureate of 1784 is deficient in is the continuity in inspiration, the regularity of taste. It is, nevertheless, admitted that this speech possesses first-rate qualities, and that seldom has philosophy of language met with a more delicate and keener interpreter.

M. Caro compares with Rivarol's speech the composition of his competitor, M. Schwab : it is slow in style, but not devoid of merit.   For M. Schwab, the cause of the universality of our tongue is a sort of natural adaptation of French taste to that of other nations in Europe.   All the advantage of such taste might possibly consist in a certain mediocrity that commends it to these nations.   Because of the originality of her national spirit, with which her tongue and her literature are, so to speak, saturated, Germany, on the contrary, meets with great obstacles to the propagation of her idiom and of her works.   The German language, says M. Schwab, will find much difficulty in becoming predominant in Europe.   Still, three circumstances might bring about such a result : 1st, The modification of the language ; 2d, The neglect of intellectual culture by the nation that speaks it ; 3d, The loss of the nation's political influence.

We must conclude with this last remark, beneath which, under pages of simple appearance, are concealed all the idea and all the hope of the good patriot Schwab.

[Report of the sitting of the " Académie des Sciences Morales et Politiques."   Extract from the paper ' Le Temps,' of 27th November 1883.]

APPENDIX J.

BIBLIOGRAPHY.

EMILE BEAUSSIRE.—The Liberty of Tuition and the University under the Third Republic. Hachette, 1883.

GASTON BOISSIER.—The Reform of Studies in the 16th Century, according to Recent Investigation. Revue des Deux Mondes, 1882.

BOUTMY.—Some Observations on the Reform of Higher Education. Paris, 1875.

MICHEL BREAL.—Pedagogic Excursions. Hachette.

COURNOT.—The Institutions of Public Instruction in France. Paris, 1864.

CH. DESMAZE.—The University of Paris. Paris, 1876.

HALMAGRAND.—Origin of the University. Paris, 1845.

HEINRICH.—French Faculties and German Universities. Lyons, 1866.

HENRI HEINE.—Germany.

HIPPEAU.—Public Instruction in Germany.

HIPPEAU.—Public Instruction in France during the Revolution. Hachette.

ERNEST LAVISSE.—Historical Teaching of the Sorbonne and National Education. Revue des Deux Mondes, 1882.

LICHTENBERGER.—The Movement of Religious Ideas in Germany. Paris, 1860.

MINSSEN.—Study on Secondary and Higher Education in Germany. Paris, 1873.

E. RENAN.—Higher Education in France, its History and its Future. Revue des Deux Mondes, 1864.

Revue Internationale de l'Enseignement. Masson, Paris.

MADAME DE STAËL.—Germany.

DR DÖLLINGER.—Die Universitäten sonst und jetzt. München, 1871.

KARL VON RAUMER.—Geschichte der Pädagogik. Deutscher Universitäts-Kalender. Winter-Semester, 1882-83.

EUG. WOLFF.—Die neue Burschenschaft. Berlin, 1880.

H. R. HAGENBACH.—Encyclopädie und Methodologie der theologischen Wissenschaften. Leipzig, 1880.—Allgemeines deutsches Commersbuch. Lahr, 1882.

FRIEDERICH UBERWEG.—Grundriss der Geschichte der Philosophie. Berlin, 1880.

O. DOLCH.—Geschichte des deutschen Studententhums. Leipzig, 1858.

THE END.

PRINTED BY WILLIAM BLACKWOOD AND SONS.

JUST PUBLISHED.

THE LIBRARY EDITION. COMPLETE IN ONE VOLUME.

DICTIONARY OF THE ENGLISH LANGUAGE, Pro-
NOUNCING, ETYMOLOGICAL, AND EXPLANATORY, Embracing Scien-
tific and other Terms, Numerous Familiar Terms, and a Copious
Selection of Old English Words. To which are appended Lists of
Scripture and other Proper Names, Abbreviations, and Foreign Words
and Phrases. By the REV. JAMES STORMONTH. The Pronun-
ciation carefully revised by the Rev. P. H. PHELP, M.A. Cantab.
Royal 8vo, handsomely bound in half morocco, 31s. 6d.

A LADY'S RIDE ACROSS SPANISH HONDURAS. By
MARIA SOLTERA. With Illustrations, post 8vo. 12s. 6d.

MADAGASCAR: ITS HISTORY AND PEOPLE. By the REV.
HENRY W. LITTLE, some years Missionary in East Madagascar.
Post 8vo, with a Map, 10s. 6d.

New and Cheaper Edition.

NORFOLK BROADS AND RIVERS; OR, THE WATERWAYS,
· LAGOONS, AND DECOYS OF EAST ANGLIA. By G. CHRISTOPHER
DAVIES, Author of 'The Swan and her Crew.' Illustrated. Crown
8vo, 6s.

New and Cheaper Edition, Revised.

A BOOK ABOUT ROSES. HOW TO GROW AND SHOW THEM.
By S. REYNOLDS HOLE, Canon of Lincoln. Eighth Edition,
Revised. Fcap. 8vo, 3s. 6d.

New and Cheaper Edition.

THE BOOK OF BALLADS. Edited by BON GAULTIER, and
Illustrated by DOYLE, LEECH, and CROWQUILL. Fourteenth Edition. Fcap. 8vo, 5s.

Sixth Edition, Enlarged.

THE MOOR AND THE LOCH. Containing MINUTE IN-
STRUCTIONS IN ALL HIGHLAND SPORTS, WITH WANDERINGS OVER
"CRAG AND CORRIE, FLOOD AND FELL;" AND RECOLLECTIONS OF
THE AUTHOR'S EARLY LIFE. By JOHN COLQUHOUN. 2 vols.
post 8vo, with Portraits, 26s.

SPORT IN THE HIGHLANDS AND LOWLANDS OF
SCOTLAND WITH ROD AND GUN. By T. SPEEDY. 8vo,
with Illustrations, 15s.

New and Cheaper Edition.

THE BABY'S GRANDMOTHER. By L. B. WALFORD,
Author of 'Troublesome Daughters,' 'Cousins,' 'Mr Smith: a Part
of his Life,' &c. New Edition, complete in one volume. Crown 8vo,
6s.

THE WORKS OF GEORGE ELIOT. CABINET EDITION.
In 20 volumes, of a convenient and handsome form, printed from a
new and legible type. £5.

CONTENTS:—Adam Bede, 2 vols.— The Mill on the Floss, 2 vols.—
Silas Marner, The Lifted Veil, Brother Jacob, 1 vol.—Scenes of Clerical
Life, 2 vols.—Felix Holt, 2 vols.—Romola, 2 vols.—Middlemarch, 3 vols.
—Daniel Deronda, 3 vols.—The Spanish Gypsy, 1 vol.—Jubal; and other
Poems, Old and New, 1 vol.—Impressions of Theophrastus Such, 1 vol.

Each Volume, price 5s., may be had separately.

NOVELS BY GEORGE ELIOT. CHEAPER EDITIONS. With
Illustrations.

Adam Bede, 3s. 6d.—The Mill on the Floss, 3s. 6d.—Felix Holt, the
Radical, 3s. 6d.—Scenes of Clerical Life, 3s.—Silas Marner, 2s. 6d.—
Romola, with Vignette, 3s. 6d.—Daniel Deronda, with Vignette, 7s. 6d.
—Middlemarch, with Vignette, 7s. 6d.

ESSAYS BY GEORGE ELIOT, AND LEAVES FROM A NOTE-BOOK.
Second Edition. Post 8vo, 10s. 6d.

WISE, WITTY, AND TENDER SAYINGS, IN PROSE AND VERSE.
Selected from the WORKS OF GEORGE ELIOT. Sixth Edition, cloth,
gilt, 6s.

THOUGHTS ON ART AND AUTOBIOGRAPHICAL ME-
MOIRS OF GIOVANNI DUPRE. Translated from the Italian by
E. M. PERUZZI, with the permission of the Author. With Portrait,
crown 8vo, 10s. 6d.

EOTHEN. By A. W. KINGLAKE. A New Edition, uniform
with the Cabinet Edition of the 'History of the Crimean War,' price
6s.

TOWARDS THE MOUNTAINS OF THE MOON. A
JOURNEY IN EAST AFRICA. By Mrs PRINGLE of Whytbank, Yair.
With a Map. 8vo, 12s. 6d.

FRENCH HOME LIFE. By FREDERIC MARSHALL. Second
Edition. Crown 8vo, 5s.

WILLIAM BLACKWOOD & SONS, EDINBURGH AND LONDON.